IT WAS
ALL RIGHT

IT WAS ALL RIGHT

MITCH RYDER'S LIFE IN MUSIC

JAMES A. MITCHELL

A PAINTED TURTLE BOOK   Detroit, Michigan

12 11 10 09 08   5 4 3 2 1

Library of Congress Cataloging-in-Publication Data

Mitchell, James A.
It was all right : Mitch Ryder's life in music /
James A. Mitchell.
  p. cm. — (Painted turtle books)
Includes bibliographical references (p. 227) and index.
ISBN-13: 978-0-8143-3337-2 (hardcover : alk. paper)
ISBN-10: 0-8143-3337-0 (hardcover : alk. paper)
  1. Ryder, Mitch. 2. Singers—Michigan—Detroit—
Biography. I. Title.
ML420.R983M57 2008
782.42166092—dc22
[B]
  2007034267

Grateful acknowledgment is made to the Leonard
and Harriette Simons Endowed Family Fund and
the Wayne State University Press Board of Advisors
Fund for the generous support of the publication of
this volume.

Designed by Isaac Tobin
Typeset by Maya Rhodes
Composed in Berthold Akzidenz Grotesk and Farnham

CONTENTS

PREFACE
A Brief Definition of "Career Biography"

This is the story of the public life and musical education of Mitch Ryder, born at age twenty in New York City and thrust into the curious cult known as American Celebrity. Ryder became famous with a string of hit records in the mid-1960s—"Jenny Take a Ride!" and "Devil with a Blue Dress On" being the most familiar songs.

It's a survivor's story and is also a story about what was survived. It's the biography of a musical career as much as it is of a musician. This is not the deeply personal, introspective story of William Levise Jr., born in Hamtramck, Michigan, in 1945, destined to find fame under another name, although that, too, is a survivor's story of personal demons and the conquering of same, some of which took place in the glow of fame's spotlight. That's a book for Levise/Ryder to write; I have as much business telling those tales as I would have singing the lead vocal on "Sock It to Me—Baby." It's not a song that other artists should attempt to "cover" (record their own version of), just as personal stories are best told firsthand.

Mitch Ryder's Life in Music, as the subtitle indicates, is an all-access pass to join Ryder on his journey through musical fame. In part, this is the story of the 1960s, a rhythm-and-blues fable of Forrest Gumpian anecdotes that gave Ryder a front-row view of the decade's twists and turns. Popular music shared the roller-coaster ride of civil rights and assassinations, war and peace signs, and—the cliché is appropriate here—drugs, sex, and rock and roll. Consider a young white man singing with a black trio when the decade of promise began, hardly aware that his was among the first Caucasian voices to mix harmonies in a still-segregated business and nation. At the decade's midpoint, Ryder heard for himself the poets who predicted that the times were-a-changing, and shared off-stage moments with artists including Jimi Hendrix and the Beatles. By the time the decade (and era) came to an end, Ryder had lost personal friends whom the public mourned from afar, victims to the very excess they pursued. Ryder was just twenty-five when the 1960s ended; his musical journey was far from over and would continue into the next century.

This project was launched by a suggestion of Ryder's: he believed he had enough "road stories" to fill a book with anecdotes from life on stage and in the spotlight. For over a year, Ryder narrated a rock-and roll travelogue that really was more than just one man's journey. It is a survivor's story, made all the more fascinating when what he survived is taken into account. If you're going to tell road stories, a description of the landscape is in order.

Most people aren't recognized internationally for things they did at twenty-one years of age (for which some of us are incredibly grateful); few are indelibly linked to a brief time when the world was their stage. Fame (musical, political, athletic, or otherwise) brings uninvited intrusion into the very matters none of us would care to share with the world. That's a private story.

What was offered to the world, in the specific case of Mitch Ryder, was more than two dozen albums' worth of recordings, upward of 8,000 performances that made people—however briefly—feel good about themselves for a while. As time went on, the familiar songs became old friends that made us dance, rock our heads, tap our feet and simply celebrate being alive.

This is the story of Mitch Ryder's life in music: the songs he sang, the times in which he entertained, and the familiar voice that reminds audiences of what they all once shared. On the whole, it was all right.

There are, of course, some people to acknowledge. A completed book is no more the effort of a single person than a record album is truly a solo project, where people are behind the control panel when even the most versatile musician is at work.

At Wayne State University Press, Jack Lessenberry and Director Jane Hoehner couldn't have been more welcoming to this project. Their enthusiasm—and others' along the way—provided immeasurable assistance in more ways than could be listed here. Copyeditor Jacqueline Kinghorn Brown greatly improved an admittedly flawed work with her sharp eye and even sharper mind. University of Michigan's American Culture Professor Bruce Conforth offered a distinguished voice for what every Detroit rock fan would like to say about Mitch Ryder. Veteran writer and producer Harvey Ovshinsky helped confirm the importance of Detroit's political and cultural scene of the early 1970s. WDIV-TV Production Manager Tom Guida was able to unearth invaluable footage toward this research—the fact that the images were captured on Beta video-recording equipment indicates the vintage of the material.

Guitarist extraordinaire Robert Gillespie provided on-stage perspective and invaluable photos, as did Leni Sinclair. Also contributing to the visual portions of this project were Robert Alford, who cast his talented eye on the Detroit Wheels reunion in the early 1980s and Ryder's time on stage with Bruce Springsteen; and Robert Matheu, determined publisher of *Creem* magazine's online rebirth. Matheu is proud to claim responsibility for the distribution of buttons bearing the challenge "Where's Mitch?" (then and now a valid question) seen at recent Rock and Roll Hall of Fame induction ceremonies. I appreciate the time taken by MC5 guitarist Wayne Kramer, whose intelligence and perspective helped guide the contents of this book; veteran guitarist Wayne Gabriel, who began and ended the 1970s on stage with Ryder, both in the band Detroit and during the 1978 return to music; disc jockey and Goose Lake promoter Russ Gibb; and rock-and-roll manager, disc jockey, and promoter Marilyn Bond.

On a personal note, neither this book nor my life would be possible without some very special individuals. My mother and father stubbornly maintained a belief in their youngest child in spite of sometimes overwhelming evidence against that conviction; my son, Alex, gives me hope for the next generation in spite of sometimes overwhelming evidence against that notion; and my significant sweetie, Linda, who made this—and pretty much everything else good about life—possible.

Of course, this project could not have done without William and Megan Levise, Mr. and Mrs. Mitch Ryder (and Dexter). I sincerely thank them for their hospitality, kindness, and trust, not to mention the occasional oatmeal cookie.

And to Mitch, on behalf of everyone who has ever turned up the volume and hit the accelerator while prowling Woodward—with "Devil" or "Jenny" blasting our soundtrack—thanks for the music, man. It was more than just "all right."

FOREWORD

Mitch Ryder

When this book is released, I will have been in music professionally for more than 47 years. In the beginning of my career, I "went to school" with many of the Detroit artists who eventually became famous in America and overseas. But at the time we didn't really think about that. We simply wanted to learn our craft and make music.

Many of the people I came to know—once I had achieved fame in America—would not live through the pressures, disappointments, spiritual and material theft, and inhumane treatment of the music industry. Some would not survive. But they were beautiful and talented and creative, and we would be worse off today had we never known their song.

At certain levels of achievement it sometimes becomes quite easy to consider some concerts as insignificant. But for me, no matter what condition I was in, once I hit the stage I became a window into my life. Perhaps there were times when it was not pretty, but I sensed that, for the audience, any evening would be a special night.

There is a side of Mitch Ryder—a very personal story—that I am pouring my heart and soul into and that will one day become my autobiography. The book you will read now is an extremely accurate account of my public, musical life. Therefore, it becomes an essential piece of the puzzle necessary to define the whole Mitch Ryder.

Originally this book was conceived as a collection of "road stories." Its author, Jim Mitchell, soon discovered these road stories were actually an account of my public life in music. For over a year I have shared some of these anecdotes with him. These are stories often told to other musicians or family or sometimes even to the public from the stage. People have told me there should be a book of these stories, and now there is. Enjoy the memories, because they are true and entertaining.

OVERTURE

The First Road Story

Before taking what may be the perfect stage name for a rhythm-and-blues singer from Detroit, Mitch Ryder saw what life on the road of music could offer. He also discovered that success in the entertainment business wasn't just about the sound of a voice.

Ryder learned those lessons before he graduated from high school, where he wasn't exactly a star student in the conventional sense. Instead, the stage and a microphone were his classroom and textbook. Friends, teachers, his father, and a minister who owned a small gospel record label were among those who took note of the obvious fact that he could sing. Different people had different ideas about what could be done with that talent.

For Ryder, it was the applause. That was the drug that offered the greatest high. As with any longtime user, Ryder clearly recalls (and still works for) the sensation he felt when he first provoked an audience response. He was fifteen; the song was "Chances Are," a soulful ballad eternally linked to the silken voice of Johnny Mathis.

In hindsight, Ryder recalled a long pause between the end of his first stage show, and the reaction. "Right after finishing, there wasn't a response from the audience," he said. He claims it was a silence lasting five, maybe six seconds; doubtful, but time often creeps slowly when you're waiting for something.

Then it hit, the noise of applause. It seemed to start with one person, but soon everyone was doing it—clapping hands, yelling, cheering. It was a crowd, a group, coming together in shared response.

"I realized there was something very powerful about what I had just done," Ryder said. "But I didn't realize how powerful it would be—people reacting to my voice."

He was in the tenth grade, with some ideas about what his future might hold. Ryder was patiently waiting for a reply from the Disney studios, where he had sent his artwork with an application for animation school. He was accepted, but by the time the letter arrived the following year his path in life had been determined.

Ryder was well aware of his other ability and passion; so were others. Warren High School music teacher Del Towers entered the sophomore in a tri-county music tournament. Ryder's victory earned him enrollment in a music camp.

He was hooked. Ryder sang whenever and wherever he could. He harmonized with a young trio, the Peps (and was often the lone pale face in the room or club). He also formed the obligatory high-school band more at home in a garage than on stage.

Before long, Ryder was encouraged to record his voice, and took his first small taste of both sides of the music business. William Levise Sr., a former Big Band–era singer whose voice was briefly heard on Detroit radio stations in the late 1940s, arranged for studio time. The father's estimation of his son's talent was shared by the ironically named Rev. James Hendrix (not the last James Hendrix to be in Ryder's life). Hendrix owned a small gospel record company, and two songs were recorded, one each written by Hendrix and Ryder.

In Ryder's mind, putting his voice on record was not the same accomplishment as earning applause during a live gig. Certainly not after he learned how the game was sometimes played. In a city that clearly knew the business of music, Ryder's modest beginnings included a glimpse at the marriage of art and commerce.

Ryder was taken to Detroit station WJLB and ushered into the control room. The men who brought the teenage singer to the studio spoke with a disc jockey about the record Ryder made. Yes, they were told, it would be played on the air. In fact, the announcer would spin the single within the hour, and they could hear it on the radio for themselves.

Anxious to get to the car and turn on the radio, Ryder was first to the door. He looked back, saw the men shake hands; money was palmed with limited discretion.

"It took away the magic," Ryder remembered. "It broke my heart. I thought I was about to get a record played on the merits of the music." It was, he said, "A very bitter pill to swallow."

At a much younger age, Ryder had seen what a particular lifestyle and certain attractions could cost a person. "The first road story," he calls it.

While still a preschool-age boy, Ryder and his older sister, Nina, were staying overnight with their grandparents, a not uncommon practice in the close family. Ryder said the arrangement gave his mother and father "private time to make more babies," an understandable speculation by one of eight children.

One winter night, it was just the young "soul mates"—Billy and Nina— keeping company with their grandparents. In the truest tradition of a factory town, Grandpa Antonio was delayed, again, in coming home from work.

In spite of the biting winds and frozen sidewalks, Ryder's grandmother obeyed another time-tested custom: wives fetching their husbands from the corner bar.

"It was just horrid out," Ryder said. "Ice, sleet, snow." They hit the road, heading down McNichols to the Paris Café, a name that inflated its purpose. It was a working-man's bar in a working-man's town: jars offered pig knuckles on the counter; sawdust-smooth shuffleboard tables; dartboards with surrounding pinholes giving the target circle a wide, dot-ted frame; neon signs winking colorful come-ons for one brand of beer or another.

Women from "the old country" did not enter such places, so Billy and Nina were sent inside to get their spirited grandfather; Their errand and purpose were quickly forgotten.

Introductions were in order, and Antonio proudly showed off his beloved grandchildren. Billy and Nina were perched on stools, tempted with orange sodas, and bribed with a lesson or two on the shuffleboard table. Antonio said it would be just another minute; there was one more thing to see, someone else to meet.

"We had no concept of time," Ryder said. "We were sitting at the bar having our second soda, and then we remembered Grandma outside."

Ryder laughed at the image, the kind of joke that only comes from a painful truth. They raced to look out the window.

"There she stood, ice hanging off her face," Ryder said. "She looked about two minutes from death."

The situation was brought to Antonio's attention. "Oh, God," he said. "We gotta go."

Outside, the Michigan winds raged. The grandparents were silent as young and old boots crackled through the ice and snow on what Ryder called "my first death march."

It's a road story of sorts, about life away from home and where that can lead. Ryder learned the ease with which those you love can be momentarily forgotten, the speed with which time can pass without a thought. "It taught me a lot about manipulation, and caring for people, and the importance of family."

He remembers that moment often. It's one of the lessons he took to New York and carried with him during his long life on the road. Ryder's voice would be heard on car radios for years, with songs that long outlived their initial moment of fame.

The price for getting those records played, though, took different forms than the cash slipped to a local disc jockey. Ryder's journey included fame and being among the celebrated in America. There's a different price to be paid for being famous.

William Levise Jr. went to New York in 1964 and became Mitch Ryder. He became known by a different name, but he always knew where he had come from.

"My mother told me to be my own person, so that I would always have that," he explained. "I go on the road now and see a lot of combinations of Temptations, or Coasters, that aren't the same guys. But there's only one Mitch Ryder, and that's cool. I think my mother would like that."

PART ONE

FROM DETROIT, MICHIGAN . . . MITCH RYDER

CHAPTER ONE

THE SOUNDS OF DETROIT

Then she put on a Detroit station,
Couldn't believe she heard it at all
She started dancing to that fine, fine music,
Her life was saved by rock and roll
In spite of the complications
She could listen to the rock and roll station
And it was all right.

    "Rock and Roll," as recorded by Detroit. . . with Mitch Ryder

His first acknowledged crime, of a sort, could be described as breaking and entering.

Five-year-old Billy Levise didn't think about his illegal act in technical terms, such as "trespassing on federal property." Telling the story decades later to the *New York Times,* he described it, "Penetrating security."

Call it a wartime excuse. America's geographical knowledge that year

9

expanded to include a place in southeastern Asia called Korea, where a three-year involvement by the United States had just begun. A military base was (and always is) intriguing to little boys.

The Levise family lived in Warren, just north of the Detroit border, at Eight Mile Road. In 1940 a tank assembly plant was built along Van Dyke Avenue—one of the principal arteries running north from the inner city—and the town that built America's cars lent its talents to the impending war. During times of conflict, backbreaking, soul-crushing assembly-line work was done with an added sense of patriotism.

Seen through the eyes of small boys, the bland, brick building painted a shade of green found only on Army structures was nowhere nearly as impressive as the fully functioning tank—a *real* tank—that faced the street, its barrel poking at the southbound Van Dyke traffic like an enormous, high-caliber hood ornament.

The decision to gain entry was an inspired moment. "My first big thrill," Ryder called it. The mission itself took plenty of work. The boys spent a half hour digging a hole under a reasonably secluded section of fence—enough to allow a child to squeeze through with his trusty bike. (One must be mobile while penetrating security.)

"We dragged our little bicycles through and took off, with the MPs chasing us," Ryder recalled. "We were so small, maybe they thought we were Korean spies. They were chasing us like mad, and we were just little guys afraid for our lives."

They were caught, of course, and the memory of the excitement stayed longer, stronger than the inevitable parental punishment that followed. Billy learned that actions have consequences, but he never forgot the rush of adventure, of poking through a barrier into unknown worlds.

Excitement came with a price, though; like the time he discovered and destroyed William Sr.'s beloved collection of records—testaments to the Big Band sounds that the elder Levise once sang on Detroit radio.

"I remember my father lying in bed and singing along with the radio for a long, long time," Ryder said. "He was crooning, mostly ballads that were popular at the time; he did it so much it went from being awesome to annoying."

Seven-year-old William Levise Jr. (Photo courtesy of Mitch Ryder.)

A preschool-age Billy found his father's record player and collection of carbon-based albums. For whatever motivates a four-year-old to act . . . well, like a four-year-old . . . the boy somehow destroyed many of the 78-rpm records.

"Oh, was he mad," Ryder remembered with a laugh, as only the distance of decades allows. "I got a lickin'. That was my first suggestion that music could also bring pain. I made a direct link between that spanking and the music. It's like Pavlov."

Music was a frequent part of the Levise household, either owing to William Sr.'s younger dreams or as home entertainment in the pre-television era. Ryder's mother, Jane Lucille McDaniel, favored the country songs of her southern youth, and the daytime radio stations supplied background music for the growing household. In the early 1940s, Ryder's mother joined the wartime migration north, to the industrial cities of promise (Cleveland, Toledo, Detroit), which the next generation would refer to—not always fondly—as the Rust Belt. Detroit welcomed anyone willing to spend his days wrestling with steel and iron, never promising an easy living and usually fulfilling that offer.

William Levise Jr. was born on Feb. 26, 1945, in Hamtramck, an island community within the boundaries of Detroit. When Billy was committing five-year-old security penetrations, the city that symbolized the industrial version of the Great American Dream was at its peak of 1.8 million people, the nation's fifth largest at the midpoint of the century. Each passing decade after the population shifted, the suburbs grew farther and farther away. This migration reflected the national baby boom–inspired escape from congested cities; in Detroit, the destination (of what some call "white flight") was to clearly marked territories. By the end of the century, the greater metro area would be the most segregated of America's big cities.

The Levise family joined the rush for suburban air, where homes sprouted up at an alarming rate to welcome the largest generation in American history. Billy and his sister, Nina, were the first of what would become eight surviving children (a ninth child was stillborn), a daunting tribe to feed on a factory worker's wages.

"There was no thought from the working-class point of view as to how the hell you were going to support them," Ryder said of the typically large families. "Every time another mouth came, we would all deal with less and less."

As a student ready to become a teenager, Billy Levise found his strongest inspirations outside of the classroom, from sources other than textbooks. His 11-year-old ears perked up when he heard an oddly understandable (to his ears) chant: "Wop bop-a-loo bop, wop bam boom."

Richard Penniman wasn't just talking about ice cream in his 1956 song "Tutti Frutti." As Little Richard, he "whoo-ed" the kids with a string of hits that strongly influenced a generation of future rockers: "Long Tall Sally," "Send Me Some Lovin'" and a lively pair of tunes praising girls named "Jenny" and "Miss Molly."

The sound made sense to the future Mitch Ryder, entering his teen years just as the term "teenager" was being redefined. As America's cultural definitions changed, music spoke the new language being heard. Little Richard, Chuck Berry, and James Brown translated jazz and rhythm and blues with electric flair; a truck driver from Tupelo, Mississippi, named Elvis Presley shook up the conventions of country, bluegrass, and (not inconsiderably) gospel. People started calling it "rock and roll," and the "babyboom" generation was challenged to explain—or fulfill—its definition.

This new sound, particularly the version generated by Little Richard and other black artists, was a foreign language that Ryder somehow understood, an awareness that hit the moment he heard it. In hindsight, he compared the feeling to a scene in the 1979 film *The Jerk,* when Steve Martin's raised-by-blacks whiteboy heard, for the first time, music he understood. "It was like that, only in reverse," Ryder said. The soul, rhythm, and exclamations, including "Have mercy!" and "Good golly!" struck a somehow familiar chord with Ryder. It was a language he planned to master.

Ryder was a student at Warren High School when the 1960s officially became a decade. Some of his interests were found in art class, where he demonstrated talent worthy of an application to study animation at the Disney studios. At the start of his sophomore year, Ryder sent them a portfolio of his work with hopes of finding a career drawing cartoons.

By the time the reply was received at the end of the academic year, Disney's offer to study the craft of cartoons was too late. "I had already made my choice," he explained. Ryder had other interests, which he pursued in partnership with Joe Kubert, his best friend from junior high school.

Kubert had grown up in nearby Troy, at the time a less-developed semirural suburb north of Detroit. Kubert's father, like Ryder's, had a musical background as a keyboard player. The two had many shared interests, but Ryder was initially impressed by the difference between the Kubert home and his own family's cramped quarters.

"I thought they were rich because they had a brick house and a manicured lawn. At that point in Troy, you had an acre-and-a-half between houses. Where I was living, when you opened your window you got splashed by the neighbor's toilet."

Undersized, mutual outcasts, the boys were not destined for fame on the athletic fields or in school popularity contests. They were, however, determined to find a creative outlet for their talents—and girls—preferably not in that order. In one memorable attempt, both purposes were put to a test when they tried out for the cheerleading squad.

"We were looking to get laid," Ryder laughed. "We were so desperate. All the hot girls were cheerleaders, so we said, 'Let's go try out.' It was too advanced a thought at the time for Warren High School."

An otherwise average student, the talents Ryder did possess were not unnoticed or unused. He wrote the Fuhrman Junior High School song while a student there, and at Warren High School teacher Del Towers not only schooled Ryder in the fundamentals of reading and writing music under classical guidelines but also encouraged the student to explore his vocal limits in other formats.

"I loved music so much I was willing to sing anything, just to get heard," Ryder said. "I was singing semiclassical and getting awards for it, but my passion was clearly with rhythm and blues."

Briefly, he formed a band with Kubert, a budding guitar player. Named the Tempest, the group lasted as long as most of the thousands of bands launched in the nascent days of rock and roll; a few rehearsals filled with more intentions than arrangements.

"We had an accordion player whose mother promised she would get him a piano," Ryder said. "She reneged on that promise, and the group broke up."

Ryder was too busy to bemoan the end of the Tempest; he was becoming familiar with the small stage at the Village, a club on Detroit's Woodward Avenue. In front of adult, paying audiences, he performed as "Billy

Lee" often enough to become comfortable on the stage, under the lights. Coupled with winning a tri-county singing contest held through school, Ryder's father looked for ways to encourage the son's talent.

A coworker of William Sr.'s belonged to a church presided over by Rev. James Hendrix, a part-time music producer who owned Carrie Records, a small, independent label which distributed a handful of modest gospel recordings. In 1962, Ryder recorded a single, "That's the Way It's Going to Be" backed with "Fool for You," composed, respectively, by Hendrix and Ryder. Ryder's contribution, among his first ventures into songwriting, was a respectful imitation of the blues ballads he was studying. The Hendrix composition "That's the Way It's Going to Be" was an attempt by the reverend to expand his gospel label into more popular directions.

"James looked around and saw Elvis and Bobby Rydell, all these white boys," Ryder said. "He thought there was a fortune to be made."

The single generated little interest. Carrie Records was not exactly in competition with Detroit's other black-owned record label, Tamla Records (later Motown), which was showing more than just a few signs of promise. The existence of an actual recording, however, began opening doors, and diverse musical ears would follow.

Hendrix wasn't the only African-American to notice that this young, small kid from just outside Detroit's boundaries sounded more like James Brown than he did white, suburban pop. In the Village, at a Highland Park basement bar called the Tantrum and at other venues, Billy Lee was building a local reputation.

"That's where I cut my teeth," Ryder said. "I ended up joining a soul act called the Peps."

In 1959 a failed boxer and ambitious songwriter borrowed about eight hundred dollars from family members and poured it into a crumbling house on West Grand Boulevard that would eventually earn the nickname "Hitsville, U.S.A." It's not bragging if you back up the claim, which the company called Motown did, over and over again.

Berry Gordy, a 29-year-old great-grandson of a slave, launched from that modest house an independent record label in pursuit of the great

American dream, urban style. Music, Gordy understood, could be the great equalizer in the quest to give African Americans a sense of place, prestige, and (as it would become known in the next decade) civil rights.

One of Gordy's early discoveries, Otis Williams (soon to form the Temptations), called Detroit "a real music town," a simple statement well understood by anyone within earshot of the countless tin speakers blasting songs from apartment windows, bar jukeboxes, and, always, car radios. Gordy's particular Holy Grail was the Hit Single, which he tried his level best to author. He cowrote several songs in the late 1950s, "Reet Petite" and "Lonely Teardrops," recorded by Jackie Wilson. The songs pulled off the previously unheard-of accomplishment of not only topping the rhythm-and-blues hit single charts but also landing "Teardrops" in the American Top Ten; the success was called "crossover," meaning a black singer had succeeded in joining Elvis and others on mainstream sales charts.

Gordy's first major discovery was a multi-talented singer and songwriter, Smokey Robinson, who led the Miracles through a string of late 1950s hits including "Shop Around" and "You've Really Got a Hold on Me." A formula developed at Hitsville—style and sophistication presented accessible melodies that demanded chart placement. In 1962, the Motown label held the No. 1 position for the first time, with "Please, Mr. Postman," a bouncy favorite by the Marvelettes, the first "girl group" in what would be one of Motown's signature sounds. On deck, Gordy was nurturing combinations that would form, re-form, and finally settle on lineups and names including the Four Tops, the Temptations, and the Supremes.

America's entertainment centers, New York and Los Angeles, took notice of this upstart company, which by 1963 had purchased the two adjoining lots and made Hitsville a description, no longer just a dream.

There were limits, though, to how much crossing-over would be allowed. Integration was less a tidal wave than determined ripples in a pond. The Supreme Court ruled in 1958 that schools should no longer be segregated, no matter how similar they seemed to be, and thereby overturned "separate but equal" as justification for the racial divide in education. However, the new experiment, desegregation and integration, was in its early days. Black faces remained a novelty in most of white America, restricted to certain venues, not welcome in many others.

The entertainment business was among the first to provide space for those with talent regardless of color. Other fields were still experimenting. Baseball, America's pastime, first allowed a black man to play with white men in 1947, when Jackie Robinson joined the Brooklyn Dodgers. In spite of a certain sense of equality on the city's assembly lines, Detroit was nearly the last team in baseball to integrate in 1958, when third baseman Ossie Virgil donned the Tigers' old English "D," cautiously taking the infield at what was then called Briggs Stadium. The city hosted one of the country's largest black populations, but a dividing line as distinct as the then-under-construction Berlin Wall existed at Eight Mile Road. Other than singing and dancing or rounding third and heading home, suburban whites had little to do with urban blacks.

Early integration in bars and music clubs was actually progressive in Detroit compared to some other regions of the country. In his biography of the Temptations, Williams recalled some of the group's earliest dates in the South, where a rope bisected the dance hall and its denizens along color lines.

Ryder didn't think in terms of "rebellion." He was simply more drawn to the gospel-influenced, sweaty sounds of rhythm and blues. The Village wasn't big enough for a rope to divide those who came to worship the music.

Ryder began working out song arrangements with three young men— a popular trio at the Village, consisting of Thomas Hester, Joe Harris, and Ronnie Abner—who performed as the Peps. There was a mutual admiration between the onstage trio and Ryder, who hung around the club begging owners Gabe and Leo Glantz for a chance to sing. The Peps invited Ryder to share a song or two, and the trio became a doo-wop, a cappella quartet. To have mixed complexions singing harmony was unusual at the time. "It wasn't flaunted because it wasn't an issue," Ryder said of the integration. He shrugged off the controversy and gave it little thought. "My mother was from the South, but she never taught me racism. My parents just weren't racist people."

The black-and-white combination was more an issue in the suburbs than the city. Ryder once invited two of the Peps for dinner with his family, an uneventful meal in the Levise household but one commented on by curious neighbors.

"When neighbors asked, 'Who were those black people?' my mother just said they were 'Billy's friends,'" Ryder said. "We didn't look at it as a bold move."

In a suburban house or on a city stage, that may have been true. In reality, the members of the Peps were too experienced to be naïve. Ryder recalled driving through Dearborn with his band mates, and when he turned to say something to his Pep passengers, they were crouched down in the back seat.

"What are you doing?" Ryder asked.

"Man, we're in Dearborn," one of the cautious, street-wise singers replied. Certain white neighborhoods had a less-than-receptive reputation, then and now.

On stage, though, there was no division between the white and black vocalists, and Ryder's reputation in Detroit clubs was of a white boy who sounded black. His was often the lone white face at Peps gigs, which ran the semiprofessional gamut of weddings, private parties, and (what Ryder counts as being among his favorite memories of the period) doing a cappella sets on the boat to Bob-Lo Island, an amusement park on the Detroit River (the watercraft journey to and from which provided as many thrills as the modest carnival rides).

Music was the introduction to a street sensibility that Ryder understood better than he did the pop-rock-prom songs dominating the soundtrack of Detroit's northern suburbs. "I just started hanging out downtown," Ryder said. "I developed a feeling for black culture because it was so much more vibrant and potent than anything else I had encountered. Somehow that black street scene just never seemed as menacing as a tank."

Before earning a driver's license, the fifteen-year-old Ryder would take the city buses away from the cheerleaders and "cruising" teenagers. He came of age in those clubs, and any peer pressure he felt came not from the high-school hallway but the stages that began featuring a pre-Temptations David Ruffin, the Four Tops and "Diane" Ross, who would later adopt the more regal sounding "Diana" when she joined the Supremes.

Suburban whites struggled with acceptance of black culture, but Ryder faced a separate challenge. "Other than at the Village, most of the people we performed for were black," Ryder said. "It was a matter of them accepting me. I think black people were more ready to accept something new and different than white people were."

In his final years at Warren High School, Ryder saw the signs of change, how urban attitudes were slipping over the Eight Mile line into the suburbs of Detroit. Adults, if they preferred, could hold tight to the image of their safe, secure bedroom communities that surrounded American cities, but then (as now) they were only fooling themselves. The kids in the school halls understood that new sensibilities, attitudes, and diversions were taking over.

"Everyone went crazy in our senior year when this kid moved into the area from Detroit," Ryder said. "He was kind of cool, very different. He stopped by the water fountain between classes and dropped an amphetamine."

Obviously a habit to be discouraged, although Ryder said there was one benefit. "In typing class he was the only one who wasn't female to get above a hundred words a minute," Ryder laughed. "He was just cranked out of his mind."

Suburban moms and dads worried about the encroachment of denim pants into a classroom culture, but fashion—as with music, language and other symbols of a generation—introduced expressions far beyond a pair of blue jeans. Some bore the colors of what attempted to be a "gang," which typically amounted to little more than a group of friends. An all-female group who called themselves the Dragons made a brief appearance at Warren High.

"They wore gang jackets to school." Ryder shook his head at the memory. "Boy, the school went nuts. I remember the heat that came down on them."

Not a gang-joining type, Ryder was more strongly influenced by the lone-guy hero image, epitomized by the television character Paladin in the series *Have Gun, Will Travel.* The experiment in clothing-with-attitude was short lived.

"I got myself all black clothes, pants, shoes. I wanted to be Paladin," Ryder said. "Walking through the halls, everyone was turning heads. After school, I got my ass kicked—very un-Paladinlike—so I stopped wearing black."

Acceptance by his peers in the always temporary world of high-school social politics was hardly a major concern: Ryder had taken his own version of the SATs on stage and listened to career counseling from outside authorities. In 1962, brothers Gabe and Leo Glantz, real-estate investors who sensed a potential gold mine in Detroit's musical talent, christened their flagship venue the Village, where Ryder was a familiar face and voice. Like the automotive proving grounds throughout the suburbs, these were the bars where bands and musicians tested their worth. As Ryder became a headliner, he took notice of others who had the proper level of talent, and the Glantz brothers—budding impresarios hoping to become the next Berry Gordy—would often pair singers with bands to see what happened.

"They would bring bands in to audition as house band," Ryder said. "They'd never pay them the first week. It was, 'See how you do with the other acts.'"

Not that becoming a regular ensured a living wage. Ryder said he earned, at the most, thirty dollars for gas money. Mostly, it was a chance to be on stage and to meet other musicians. In late 1962, guitarist Jim McCarty, bass player Earl Elliott, and drummer John "Johnny Bee" Badanjek—who was all of fourteen years old at the time—auditioned to be house band at the Village. They called themselves the Rivieras.

The three musicians were certifiable products of Detroit, growing up near the Michigan State Fair grounds off Woodward Avenue. Ryder said they shared an appreciation for the black artists of the day (both the nationally famous and their fellow local Detroiters, who would soon find the celebrated spotlight), although McCarty was clearly more influenced by the straight rock-and-roll style of Chuck Berry than the rhythm and blues of James Brown.

"They were listening to the same black stations I did," Ryder said. "But they were kind of worshiping what would become the British Invasion. The combination of my rhythm and blues sensibilities and their liking the British version of American rock and roll turned out to be pretty potent."

This trio, who were making the same rounds of clubs, whether the Village, the 20 Grand Club, or jazz/blues joints like the Minor Key, impressed Ryder.

To the audience, the acts that came and went seemed to be professional musicians. Ryder instead considered them "students trying to become stars." On the small stages of smoky bars, dance moves were perfected, song lyrics were memorized, and guitar licks became second nature. "Those are the testing grounds," Ryder said. "That's where you learn to have confidence on stage."

Music was what brought the young players and singers to the stage, but the growing success of the Motown label added another incentive. Detroit could no longer be considered solely in terms of its automobile production. The Berry Gordy empire expanded its reach in October 1962, when the first "Motor Town Revue" hit the road for a six-week tour. Headliner Mary Wells appeared over Martha and the Vandellas, the Marvelettes, Little Stevie Wonder, the Supremes, and the Temptations, taking the Detroit sound to the rest of the nation.

"We knew that Motown, and Berry Gordy, articulated that," Ryder said. "People were becoming national stars. Jack Scott appeared on *American Bandstand,* with the jeans, motorcycle boots and T-shirt."

Scott, born across the Detroit River in Windsor, Ontario, echoed the tough, street-guy persona expected from rockabilly-style singers shunned by country fans for being too raw. The singer made frequent chart appearances, peaking in 1960 with the cry-in-the-beer ballads "What in the World's Come Over You" and "Burning Bridges." Considered the first white rock-and-roller from Detroit, Scott qualified as a local celebrity, and his appearances—musical or otherwise—were local news.

Ryder heard on the radio that Scott was to appear at an A&W Root Beer stand and assumed the announcement was for an outdoor concert of some sort.

"We went to see the performance," Ryder recollected with a laugh. "Actually we found out he was there to fight somebody. There was a rumble that night. It was all about the rebellious attitude."

Rock and roll was born of rebellion—against a laundry list of targets ranging from the "system" to people over thirty to the previous conventions of music—but show business remained a business. Motown, perhaps recognizing the risk of white America accepting black entertainers, put a coat of gloss on the product in an effort to bridge the racial divide, with tuxedo-wearing men and women with straightened hair.

The feeling, though, was similar. No matter how much glitz was poured over a Detroit act—especially those singing the harmless love ballads of the day—the songs from the cities remained the sounds of blue-collar rebellion, of defiance of convention.

"It's about being bored," Ryder said. "About raising yourself above that level."

It was also about dedication to a craft and accepting the judgments of that pursuit. Some high-school students worked at jobs, either out of necessity or for that elusive entity known as "disposable income," but the employment was typically not one for which sixteen-year-olds have a passion. Ryder's extracurricular pursuits were the apprenticeship of a musician. His lessons revealed the rewards as well as the downside of chasing musical dreams.

Ryder saw what music had done to his father, a one-time Big Band singer whose love of music had been overtaken by the responsibilities of a family man.

"To be a singer kind of scared me," Ryder said. "I didn't want to be unhappy. When I joined the choir, I realized what happened to my father might not happen to me. I became more deeply involved in the music, and I decided to be a singer when I no longer feared falling into the trap my father had fallen into."

CHAPTER TWO

SONG AND DANCE

The end of his public education at Warren High School was a painful day for William Levise Jr., although not for any sentimental reasons tied to leaving his academic career behind en route to becoming Mitch Ryder.

"The day before, I had been to Pontiac Lake and gotten sunburned, and I had no clothes on under my robe," Ryder said.

A flowing robe worn under a matching mortarboard breezed in the summer wind; Ryder was effectively naked when accepting his certificate. The principal grabbed Ryder's arm—likely sending screaming shards of pain through the sunburned body—and offered a tribute to a less than stellar student.

"He said these endearing words into my ear as he handed me my diploma: 'The only reason you're getting this is because I don't want to see you next year,'" Ryder remembered. "I marched off to the future with that note of confidence."

Along with most students, Ryder was more certain of what he didn't want from life than what he expected. Post–high-school education in 1963 wasn't quite the given that it would become, and college was not in the majority of his classmates' plans. Teenage boys in factory towns were less concerned about the remote possibility of a recently initiated war in a country called Vietnam than of the more readily evident prospects of a slow, twenty-year death on the assembly line.

"There was a lot of frustration here," Ryder said of Detroit. "Nobody wanted to die making cars. There was a strong impetus to get out—and stay out—of the factory. Not that it isn't a proud way of making a living; it's just a hard way."

In hindsight, the chosen path may have been the harder of two evils. "When you're young, you fool yourself into thinking that music is going to be easier," Ryder said in a 2002 interview. "We probably ended up killing ourselves more than our fathers did on the line."

With uncertain plans beyond his next gig as Billy Lee, Ryder accompanied Joe Kubert's family on a Florida vacation. The bleached-white beaches of the Atlantic Ocean were a foreign land compared to the lakes of southeast Michigan. The vacation adventure seemed a luxury to Ryder, a middle-class indulgence that his family couldn't afford.

"I was envious, but desiring of that lifestyle," Ryder said.

Ryder and Kubert lounged on the beach, hoping to spot girls brazen enough to wear bikinis and listening to the scratchy sounds of a transistor radio. That summer, the American Top Ten was well populated with Motown acts, including "Little" Stevie Wonder's "Fingertips, (Part II)," memorable for being the first live recording to top the charts, but mostly owing to the musician being all of twelve years old. Black and white sounds showed remarkable extremes on that summer's soundtrack, from James Brown's *Live at the Apollo* album to the Surfaris' guitar classic, "Wipe Out." Attitudes ranged from Lesley Gore's pouty protest "It's My Party" to the eternally misunderstood lyrics of the Kingsmen's "Louie, Louie."

Mostly, people were talking about a new group that summer of 1963, a British quartet just starting to test the waters this side of the Atlantic.

It may have been jealousy, envy, or simply the sort of competitive spirit needed to go onstage in the first place, but Ryder was less than impressed.

"Those guys ain't shit," Ryder said to Kubert. "We can put a group together."

Coming from a competitive musician, an early dismissal of the Beatles was understandable. Other than a few fan magazine photos, the Liverpool lads had yet to be seen in the United States, and their first two singles released in this country—"Please, Please Me" in February and "From Me to You" in May 1963—didn't seem to offer anything too special or a quality that couldn't be found in America, let alone in Ryder's hometown.

"We saw the public reaction to that but really had no respect for their abilities," Ryder commented with a laugh in hindsight. "Coming from Detroit and having the need to prove yourself, that resentment was part of our fiber."

Motown Records, Ryder said, was becoming, "an image of power for all the kids in Detroit. It said to the world that something was happening in Detroit."

Impressed or not by the music—the standard three verses and chorus allowed within two and a half minutes—the initial influence of the Beatles was the sound that launched a thousand bands. Garage groups, quartets, and quintets squeezed around basement pool tables with budget-priced amplifiers that proved beyond the control of most amateur guitarists; drummers tested the patience of parents, and singers learned that amplified microphones pick up every mistake not heard while singing along with the radio.

It sure looked like fun, but it certainly was a lot of work and required talent to go with the tenacity. Ryder had already learned to hold a microphone, to sing onstage, to front a band of musicians. He had been a solo act and performed as lead singer; it was time to see if being part of a band was the way to succeed.

"We can put a group together," Ryder told Kubert, who reminded the singer of the failed experiment in junior high school that had been the

Tempest. Ryder shook his head. He had become friendly with a musical trio of actual professionals called the Rivieras: Jim McCarty, Earl Elliott, and John Badanjek.

"There's these guys I saw down at the Village," Ryder said. "They're really cool, and play rock and roll and rhythm and blues." Ryder and Kubert returned to Detroit, free from school, challenged to find a future.

"When we got back, that's when we organized," Ryder said. "That's how it started."

Drummer John Badanjek's parents both worked—the family business being a bar that required both to put in long hours—and the attic of their home became the rehearsal hall for Billy Lee and the Rivieras.

Badanjek recalled the group's origins four decades later in an interview with *Classic Drummer* magazine. Guitarist McCarty's father became friendly with the drummer's father at the bar that Badanjek described as, "a beer-and-shot joint strategically placed between the auto factories." A meeting was arranged between the thirteen-year-old drummer and the tall, thin guitar player two years his senior. (Badanjek's interest in a friendship included both the obvious guitar talent and, in no small measure, the imminent issuance of a Michigan driver's license for McCarty.) Initially, the teenagers played in each other's wedding bands—McCarty's the Debonairs and Badanjek's own Starlighters—while studying the previous generation's masters of their respective instruments. In time, Badanjek's thirteen-year-old friend Earl Elliott completed the trio, and the foundation of a band was born. A performance at the Michigan State Fairgrounds brought the nascent group to the attention of band manager George Williams III, who put the act to work in the downtown club the Village. The wide-eyed Badanjek lost count of the musicians who worked the club, from jazz greats to future members of the Temptations, but said that one singer in particular caught their attention.

"There was this kid from the suburbs—Billy Levise—singing with this black group, the Peps," Badanjek recalled. "George Williams arranged for us to get up and play [with him], and the place just got excited as hell."

Ryder and Kubert, fresh from Florida, joined the now-frequent rehearsal sessions held in what Badanjek called, "The Studio," the upstairs of a usually empty family home decorated wall-to-wall with the sleeves of 45-rpm records. As the summer of '63 faded, the boys practiced endlessly, "damn near every day," Ryder said, until their material was of sufficient quantity and quality and their act was ready to roll. If their harmonies and rhythms took time to adjust, their attitudes were consistent from the start.

"We just believed," Ryder said. "We knew we were going to be stars."

The group's repertoire included the standard ballads and crowd pleasers mandatory of any band wishing to be paid, whether the performance was at a club, concert hall, wedding, or bar mitzvah. The Beatles' early catalogue was learned, as was a selection of James Brown, Smokey Robinson, and what Badanjek called "Detroit/Soul." Somewhere in between, the translation of rock and rhythm gave birth to a sound, a language being spoken.

McCarty told *Vintage Guitar* magazine that this new music was a fusion of sorts that merged the compatible styles. "What we had in common was the rhythm and blues thing as opposed to pop Top Forty," McCarty said. "We had various musical tastes. I was listening to blues guys: B.B. King made me want to pick up a guitar."

It wasn't long before Billy Lee and the Rivieras were ready to expand their audience beyond the bars and music clubs of Woodward and Detroit, but there was no formal management for the group. Family and friends who had the time and patience to arrange club dates did what they could. William Levise Sr. tried to get the boys into a recording studio, while an acquaintance of Elliott's found places for the band to play.

There were more than enough opportunities to be found. When it came to dance floors built in the first half of the twentieth century, Detroit's working-class attitude carved its own place in American musical history through sheer size. The Bob-Lo Island Pavilion, built in 1914, boasted for a time the second largest floor in the nation, capable of bearing the steps of five thousand dancers. The same year saw construction of the Arcadia Dance Hall on Woodward Avenue. Through the Roaring Twenties Detroit built a reputation—one enormous floor at a time at venues including the Jefferson Beach Pavilion, the Greystone Ballroom, and Edgewater Park—as a city that knew what to do with live music. The Big Band-era "boom" of music halls continued into the next generation. By 1966, the Grande Ballroom on Grand River Avenue featured one of the most spacious hardwood floors in the country.

In suburban Walled Lake, an amusement park complex that did not include Las Vegas-style gambling was mislabeled "casino." Built in 1919 as a small dance hall and bathhouse by Jake and Ernest Taylor, the park's early offerings included water slides with wooden toboggans splashing riders into the lake. Through the 1930s, the Walled Lake Casino Pavilion flourished in spite of a Depression-challenged auto industry, and the floor was often filled to its 2,500 capacity. When swing was the thing, the room was popular with the Big Bands and gave the nation a taste of Detroit when performances were broadcast on national radio shows. Closed for the duration of World War II, the ballroom reemerged in 1946 as a stage suitable for Harry James, Louis Armstrong, Sammy Kaye, Guy Lombardo, and a Who's Who of swing and jazz.

The backstage walls couldn't talk, but they bore a record of music's legacy: it was customary for musicians to leave their signatures on a wall. The connection of music through the years was not lost on the young players desperate to carry the torch into a new decade.

"All those signatures, all those great names," Ryder marveled. "We felt really special to be playing in that place."

The melodies may have changed from the days when Satchmo sounded a generation's horn and clothing and hairstyles adapted to that era, but the enthusiasm of dancing remained a constant, now ready to take on an unprecedented role as symbol of a generation. Music was becoming more of an obsession than a diversion.

For some, that meant there was money to be made. Following a brief closure, the Walled Lake Casino Pavilion reopened in 1962, ready to host package shows of national and local talent put together by radio stars, including Lee Allen of WXYZ. "Little Stevie" Wonder, Chuck Berry, and Motown acts highlighted shows there. By 1964 an increasing number of multi-band concerts featured—and were dominated by—Billy Lee and the Rivieras.

The size of the ballrooms required musical adjustments. For bands in the first half of the 1960s, the equipment was the same regardless of venue. Amplifiers allowed small groups to fill the same room covered by a larger band of forty or so players, and the singer was likewise "amplified," with all sounds heading out to the audience.

One piece of equipment in particular had yet to become standard issue. "When I started there were no monitors," Ryder said of the simple yet necessary speaker that allows a singer to actually hear himself sing. Vocalists relied on experienced guesswork to find the proper key. "When the band got too loud, you were shit out of luck."

The shows offered exposure, if little else. "They wouldn't pay you anything," Ryder said. "They wouldn't even give you gas money. We ended up driving all over and borrowing money from our parents trying to make it happen."

There was more to learn about the business than just being onstage. The nature of fame, pop music, and the people involved brought other lessons. At one show, the disc jockey—a local radio announcer—asked Ryder to help him while he took care of what could be considered a personal matter.

"Listen, kid, you gotta do something," the fast-talking jockey instructed the teenage singer. "Could you spin a few records?"

Impressed by the size of the portable collection brought by the station, Ryder looked through the 45-rpm singles, selected "Cathy's Clown" by the Everly Brothers, and played the song. The announcer still hadn't returned. Ryder played the same song again. Then again and again.

A half hour later, perhaps a little longer, the announcer returned from the parking lot. "He was out in the car with a young girl," Ryder said. "He could have gone to jail if anyone checked her age. She comes in, all messed up, disheveled; he's trying to straighten his act up, and starts spinning records. I thought, 'Wow, what a business.'"

Entertainment is a business, like any other, and success takes more than just musical ability. On these proving grounds, Billy Lee and the Rivieras put together a show that was more than just music.

"I brought to the stage show all the tricks I'd seen my rhythm and blues heroes do," Ryder said. Sliding, kicking out, knee drops, partial disrobing, comedy routines. The goal was to get the most reaction from an audience, and if there was a sense of competition, all the better. Artistic appreciation might have been mutual, but when an event was called a "battle of the bands," Ryder saw no reason the Rivieras couldn't be the victors claiming the spoils.

"We relished them," Ryder said. "We went in with the intent of destroying our competition."

It hadn't taken long. The Rivieras were a well-rounded, multidimensional, all-purpose band. These weren't the confined bars of Woodward, but Ryder and the band would often treat the more cavernous spaces as they did a compact club. Ryder clearly was willing to give his all to a show.

"I did stage dives at the Walled Lake Casino," Ryder told the Detroit weekly *Metro Times* four decades later. "Except back then, nobody caught you. They'd just make room for you on the floor."

The band assumed they could put on the best show of the night, equal parts goal and belief. "We can beat those guys," Ryder told himself and the band reminded one another. Any thrill given the audience paled in comparison to the rush felt by the players. Whatever worked became part of the act. An on-stage argument that created crowd reaction was repeated in the next show, because it worked. As often as not, routines were born of accident. Badanjek came out from behind the drum kit to dance during an instrumental break, attempted an assisted back-flip, and accidentally knocked Ryder out with a kick. A comedy skit developed from trying to revive the singer. Variations were tested: "See what happens if I don't get up," Ryder said of this experiment. The show must go on—and always did.

The audience included more than just music fans or young dancers in search of an excuse to let it all hang out. Wayne Kramer was a budding high-school guitar player years away from cofounding the MC5 and in

Profile of a band: Billy Lee and the Rivieras, 1964. (Photo from the Robert Matheu Collection.)

search of local inspiration that didn't include a British accent.

"I'd been hearing about this group through the grapevine in the world of bands," Kramer said. "They had a regular job at a place called the Bamboo Hut, and they were incredible." In response to the teenage appetite for the rock-and-roll menu, Kramer said a number of "Teenage Night Clubs" sprouted throughout the Metro Detroit area, where soda was served renamed to sound like cocktails. Kramer frequented these clubs with his friends and quickly became fans of Billy Lee and the Rivieras.

"It was set up like a bar," Kramer said. "Me and all the guys who later became the MC5 went down to see them, and we were universally blown away."

There was a lot to like, from Kramer's perspective. The group dressed well, fashionably but avoiding the Liverpool-mandated "uniforms." Musically, Kramer took notice of, "this skinny, young, pimply-faced drummer who just played his heart out." As a future guitarist himself, Kramer was particularly impressed with McCarty's handling of the instrument.

"They started each set with instrumentals that featured Jim McCarty's guitar playing," Kramer said. "McCarty was really an extraordinary player in those days; he just had a superior technique. I was impressed especially with his speed. He could play sixteenth-notes and really fast triplets. I remember saying, 'I gotta learn how to do that.'"

Also appreciated by Kramer was the choice of material. Billy Lee and the Rivieras obligingly covered the conventional hits of the day (Beatles, Beach Boys) for their suburban fans but also attacked riskier—not to mention risqué—selections.

"They played material that was all of our favorite songs," Kramer said. "They played James Brown's 'Please, Please, Please,' and did it credibly. Years later, in the MC5, we also covered James Brown material. I actually don't think we did it as well as the Rivieras."

Kramer said the Rivieras inspired him to not just learn his musical instrument but also to find a practical application for his talent. "The impression they left me with really informed my thinking about what it means to be a musician and to be in a band and perform for people in night clubs," Kramer said. "They were cool, they sounded great, they looked great, and they played in nightclubs. That's all I ever wanted. They were everything I wanted to be."

Of course, backstage personalities sometimes found their way into the spotlight. Ryder said that bass player Elliott was, in reality, angry with him one night. The choreographed section of the revive-the-singer skit in which Elliott was to loosen Ryder's necktie didn't go as planned.

"He kept pulling it, and put his foot on my neck. I'm turning beet red while he gets his revenge," Ryder said and laughed. "Man, I hate when you have those family fights in public."

The way the Rivieras saw it, they might as well have fought each other. They held the unofficial crown of Kings of Local Band Battles.

"We had nobody left to beat," Ryder said. Early Motown stars played the Casino, but in the summer of 1964 Billy Lee and the Rivieras were the headliners.

"It wasn't just, 'Stand up there and sing'; for us it was show time," Ryder said. "The real show the kids came to see was us."

Before long, it wasn't just the kids wanting to see this new act, not in a business that perpetually seeks the undiscovered version of previous success.

New Jersey–born Bob Crewe began composing songs in the early 1950s (with cowriter Frank Slay) and turned to producing while harboring his own ambitions as a performer. Heading into the 1960s, Crewe connected with the right people at the right time. Now teamed with Bob Gaudio, Crewe wrote "Sherry," "Big Girls Don't Cry" and the early-1963 chart-topper, "Walk Like a Man," ably recorded by Frankie Valli and the Four Seasons, a Crewe-produced success. By the time the Beatles shook up America with their February 1964 appearance on the *Ed Sullivan Show,* hit-makers and producers saw themselves as the next Brian Epstein or Berry Gordy.

Crewe wanted to break new talent and was in a receptive mood when a tape arrived featuring a half-hour's worth of frenzied rhythm and blues, a harsh, white-sounding rock and roll with a black-inspired voice demanding attention. It was rehearsal tape of Billy Lee and the Rivieras, touted as local stars determined to reach the next level. The basement recording included "Lucille" and other highlights from their stage show.

The tapes weren't the only recordings made by Billy Lee and the Rivieras; a 1964 single was financed by Ryder's father and released on the local Hyland label. "You Know," backed with "Won't You Dance with Me," was released in the Detroit area, received modest airplay, but was destined to remain a record for local ears only.

The band had supporters, though, who saw them going beyond the Detroit area. Disc jockey Dave Prince sent the basement rehearsal tape to Crewe in New York. Crewe was intrigued but knew he had to see the band onstage before making any commitment. In late 1964, Billy Lee and the Rivieras were hired to open for the Dave Clark Five, among the early wave of the British Invasion, at the Masonic Temple Auditorium. Crewe was in the audience, first-hand witness to a crowd that wildly encouraged a planned fifteen-minute show into nearly an hour of frenzied music.

It was an inspired performance in more ways than one. Ryder and the band had grown tired of the mania that coattailed the Beatles and then attached itself to virtually any British group washing ashore in America. In the months following the Beatles' appearance on *Ed Sullivan,* they held the Top Ten door open—usually from the top position—to any number of other groups sporting familiar-looking haircuts.

Disc jockey Russ Gibb joined the on-air crew at Detroit's WKMH (the station's call letters later became WKNR, or "Keener" to Motor City motorists) in the pivotal year 1963 and shared Midwest America's cynicism for many of the redcoat-tail groups, who seemed to have had an easy entry to stardom. "The English mystique arrived in America," Gibb said. "The Beatles had been on *Ed Sullivan,* and the media were jumping on the English thing." Within the industry, Gibb noticed that promoters, record labels, and managers were more interested in imported talent than in homegrown sounds, regardless of quality.

"We started to get a lot of English groups that really wouldn't have made it in America had they not been brought here and promoted like hell," Gibb said. "There were a lot of American groups that were better."

That perception didn't go unnoticed by the musicians. "They had a free ride in the beginning," Ryder said. "All they were doing was grooming everybody to be like the Beatles, covering black music and wearing their hair a certain way."

It was a safe bet that the screaming horde of teenage girls who surrounded the Auditorium was there to see the cute English boys. Backstage in the dressing room, the Detroit natives were taking it personally.

"We had these little slat windows," Ryder said of backstage accommodations. "We opened the window to get some air, and someone saw one of our hands and started screaming."

The band members themselves knew that Billy Lee and the Rivieras did not cause the sexually charged response. "They think we're fucking British!" Ryder screamed. The band was pissed off, and pumped. It couldn't have been a better time to be called onstage.

"We went into our show and did everything that worked," Ryder said. "The jumping, the stripping, the whole routine. The music was pounding; we just wouldn't stop. The little girls knew what was going on."

So did the people who earned their living by knowing what little girls—and teenage guys—wanted from music. Marilyn Bond was a disc jockey, concert promoter, and manager of local talent (promoting appearances by stars including Bobby Darin, who helped discover Jamie Coe and the Gigolos, regional garage-rock heroes who were managed by Bond.) Bond knew that Crewe—hardly alone in his perception—made frequent weekend visits from New York to Detroit in search of talent; the city's reputation was growing with each Top Ten record released by Motown, its stars learning early and well the value of showmanship behind the music.

"I'd seen a whole load of entertainers 'make it,'" Bond said of her initial impressions of Billy Lee as front man to the Rivieras. "He stood out. If there was a balcony in the theater, he'd slide down from the balcony to the stage. Who's going to have the guts to do that? If you're really an entertainer, you keep what works. Those are the ones who make it." The combination of Ryder's vocal and stage talent and Crewe's flair with show business, Bond said, "was a double-whammy." Bond knew Ryder would soon face a choice: to remain a local sensation or to take a chance with Crewe. Hardly a challenging decision, Bond said, given Crewe's track record.

The show that Ryder now calls "The Night We Destroyed the Dave Clark Five" was everything Bob Crewe was looking for. Crewe extended his stay in Detroit, coaxing management-contract signatures out of five sets of overwhelmed parents. Having watched the industry carefully in recent years, the bandsmen and their families were impressed with the opportunity.

"The guy could have had anyone," Ryder said. "He had all these hits with the Four Seasons. To take an interest in us was a credit and a compliment. We said, 'What's next?' We were hungry enough to eat America. But we didn't know there was a limit to what you could eat."

As 1964 came to a close—a year America mourned for a slain president and was reminded via Southeast Asia of a generation's possible mortality— Billy Lee and the Rivieras were invited to the table of popular fame.

"We were asked to go to New York, and we jumped at the chance," Ryder said.

CHAPTER THREE

COME ALONG WITH ME

Five guys, four beds, and one bathroom: Welcome to the big city, boys. On Manhattan's Upper West Side, the Coliseum House at 71st Street and Broadway was the destination for a band of overwhelmed teenagers, delivered by several taxis' worth of songs to be played and the basic equipment to start playing them, a group whose senior member was still not finished with his teenage years.

The size of the city was amazing. Detroit was more sprawl-oriented (especially in the early days of suburban escape), but New York was huge. Everything aimed at the sky with aggressive determination. "Bigger" was the unofficial motto of an island whose shadows were cast from so many stories above; an endless competition in Times Square tried for the most light bulbs in a single billboard; Grand Central Station itself, which welcomed the band, was cavernous and dwarfed most venues played by Billy Lee and the Rivieras.

For such a big city, though, hotel rooms could be impressively small:

two cramped rooms with twin beds. Making music together in front of an audience was one thing. It was time to see if they could live together—and have a future—as a group.

The first order of business, even before finding a new name, was to determine who would be assigned to sleep on the sofa. (Teenage guys don't typically share a bed.) The initial plan was for a democratic rotation; each musician taking his due turn. In the predictable nature of group politics, that didn't last long. Rhythm guitarist Joe Kubert drew the short straw most nights.

"We started isolating Joe for whatever reason," Ryder said. It hardly mattered, given the accelerated changes that would take over their lives. The hotel mostly served as a dressing room before taking the stage.

Those first weeks were cautious times. No matter how street smart Detroit made a young man, southeast Michigan doesn't prepare someone for New York. Most places can't, and the city allows Americans to experience culture shock right in their own country. The group's members weren't eager to venture too far away from the Coliseum, at least not in the early days. A rotating buddy system was worked out, as arbitrary as the room assignments. "We teamed up to face the cruel world out there," Ryder said.

And learn to deal with each other in close quarters. In the Coliseum, Ryder initially shared one of the small rooms with Jim McCarty, whose dedication to his craft was admirable, but he wasn't easy to live with. They would come back to the rooms from closing one club or another, the night hours reaching closer to morning, but McCarty wasn't ready to call it a day.

"Jimmy would start listening to these jazz records," Ryder said. "That would go on for a couple of hours. Then he'd pick up his guitar and start practicing."

Personality quirks became evident. Drummer Johnny "Bee" Badanjek had more than a slight touch of claustrophobia. They learned this when he was locked in a room by the other four (another game played in rotation). Badanjek panicked and broke down the door to escape, a practical joke that gave the band their first trashed-hotel-room story (predating the antics of the Who's Keith Moon by several years).

With bass player Earl Elliott, Ryder teamed briefly with a roommate who sprinkled baby powder between the sheets before getting into bed. "That was kind of weird," Ryder said.

Perhaps, but no more so than the ways the band members found to occupy themselves, kill time, and seek an outlet for teenage energies that would soon be unleashed on stages and in recording studios.

They were creative, though, whether at work or play.

"One night we took the microphones and an amplifier to the roof of the hotel," Ryder said. The performers addressed the crowded streets below. "We tried to warn them of an alien invasion, but none of them spoke English."

Some of the passersby probably figured out the joke anyway, if they assumed that the same crew had been responsible when hundreds of paper airplanes landed in the neighborhood. It didn't take long, however, for their playground to expand, and there wouldn't be time or energy to manufacture a fleet of paper aircraft. Producer Bob Crewe's connections opened the doors, and the band's music clinched the deal. The group quickly became a working act. They made a name for themselves in Greenwich Village clubs and Times Square bars, both as a house band and playing behind some legendary talent.

The name they took to the New York stages, however, was not Billy Lee and the Rivieras. A group called the Rivieras had recorded "California Sun," and they didn't want to risk confusion, either by the public or in court. A new name was needed.

For inspiration, they started looking at random names in the Manhattan telephone directory. They discarded several choices before finding one that made sense the moment it presented itself.

With Mitch Ryder front and center, what else could the band be called but the Detroit Wheels?

They learned fast: the music scene, the culture of New York, and the business of making a living onstage. The lessons were accented by their youth—so young that Badanjek didn't qualify for a cabaret license, given the requirement that bar musicians be at least sixteen years of age. "It was a problem until we figured out how to . . . just fake it, lie about it," Ryder said.

The Wheels were unconcerned about their drummer being a few months' shy of sixteen, but the reason for the license requirement had more of an impact on their lives as musicians. "We were used to doing teen dances in Detroit," Ryder said. "But these were adult clubs—bars, saloons—and a lot of drinking, which in Detroit we had only experienced at bar mitzvahs."

Three sets a night, five nights a week—that's how bands learn their craft. Guitar chords become second nature; drum cadences grow to be as natural as breathing; and pacing enables the singer's voice to last for an evening. The Wheels had paid their dues in Detroit, learning to rock the house or deliver requests for someone's favorite song.

In New York, a little cultural diversity was a smart tool to have at their disposal. "Some big spender came in one night," Ryder said, "a Jewish man. He wanted to hear 'Hava Nagila.' Of course, we had played so many bar mitzvahs, we knew the song." To clinch the deal, the man offered a hundred dollars for the performance, a sum agreed to after a brief conversation between the singer and the customer.

After the show, it was time for payday. "We had an argument over how it was going to be divided," Ryder said. "The drummer had a certain demand, because he and the guitar player had taught the other two the song. I had my idea of what should happen, because I was singing it and I made the deal."

Opinions were offered. Two of the musicians sought preferential earnings because they had arranged dates for that night. "The hundred dollar argument lasted a half hour," Ryder wryly observed.

However it was divided, Ryder recalled the moment because of its relative innocence, a debate that could have easily been between boys on a playground deciding the batting order for a pickup game. He remembered the spirit of simplicity, the way all nostalgia is recalled, as a period that didn't last long.

The original Detroit Wheels (*left to right*): Jim McCarty, Earl Elliott, Mitch Ryder, John Badanjek, and Joe Kubert. (Photo from the Robert Matheu Collection.)

The perfect grid of Manhattan's crossstreets and endless avenues loses its definition below 14th Street; the trails of Greenwich Village offered more to choose from than simply turning left or right. Narrow roads—some retaining the same cobblestones that horse-drawn carriages once clopped over—snaked through an ever-changing mix of shops and restaurants and nightclubs, specialty stores, newsstands, and apartments. On the streets, pedestrians ruled the old-fashioned way, through sheer numbers drawn from an endless dance of sidewalk living and bohemian dreams.

The Village has a soundtrack, felt if not always heard from basement bars on Fourth Street, Bleecker Street, Eighth Avenue, and every other spoke in the distorted wheel. In 1965, the sounds heard from dozens of clubs played a mongrel creature born of rock and roll, a hybrid of folk, jazz, blues, and something indefinable. Sometimes it was played for sheer electric volume; other times as strumming background to protest poetry.

The Wheels became club regulars at Trude Heller's, a Village fixture on Sixth Avenue that was very much the domain of its namesake owner. "An old dyke with a fantastic personality," Ryder fondly recalled. Heller had found considerable success, as had her son, Joel, owner of the nearby Eighth Wonder, which also became an occasional date on the Wheels' calendar. "He was quite a character," Ryder said. "He didn't have a father, and his mom was a lesbian. He was a little confused."

The sexual orientation of some Village residents—certainly more per capita than the Wheels knew existed in the early-1960s Midwest—wasn't the only rude awakening for the boys. When they headlined Detroit hops and dances, the "worldly wise" young men walked the self-assured strut of boys who believed themselves knowledgeable—even experienced—in sexual matters.

But they hadn't walked around Greenwich Village. Their home-base club was located near a residence for women who were a little more experienced, and outspoken, than the teenage girls who screamed at bands in suburban venues.

"The club was across from a female prison," Ryder said. "I remember walking to work every night in the summer, and the women would hang out the window and yell all these weird things to us." The gauntlet was an educational walk in many ways, adding to the eye- and ear-opening atmosphere. "We had no idea that women could actually talk the way they talked." Ryder shook his head at the suggestions made by the bored inmates. "The things they said they were going to do to our little teenage bodies just boggled our minds."

When the Wheels weren't playing Heller's, they visited or performed at dozens of clubs, where reputations were growing for names like Simon and Garfunkel, Peter, Paul, and Mary, and other newcomers to the pop scene. One year earlier, a demonstration of both style and potential substance was given by the Beatles, and new boundaries for lyrics were explored by Bob Dylan. The next few years would change far more than just a musical genre.

It was an explosive scene of artists, all aiming for the brass ring of stardom. No matter the path they chose to take, there was reason to believe that their sound—whatever sound that was—would find a home among the songs being consumed by a public with diverse tastes. When Ryder and the Wheels moved to New York, the Top Ten records on the *Billboard* magazine sales chart included the Righteous Brothers' soulful aria, "You've Lost That Loving Feeling"; Petula Clark's ironically bouncy ditty, "Downtown"; and "My Girl," the Temptations' candidate for the perfect single.

Some were obvious in their quest for a mania-inspired pop song, groups of the Herman's Hermits or Freddie and the Dreamers variety. The pop charts always had room for catchy tributes to teenage love.

But others were less obvious, revealing more sophisticated imagery and references. The Byrds landed a Top Ten hit with "Mr. Tambourine Man," a Bob Dylan composition said to be inspired by a drug dealer in the Village's landmark Washington Square Park. The times, the man said, were "a changin'." These weren't the teenage records played in suburban Detroit just a few months earlier; the audience at Trude Heller's was a world apart from the fans Ryder and the Wheels had made dance in Detroit.

The stage at Heller's was small, barely big enough for a singer to stand in front of a crowded drum kit. Under skeletal lighting with a minimum amount of equipment, Ryder and the Wheels were flanked by ever-present dancers at each side of the stage. The band cranked out three nightly sets, five nights a week. During the early winter months, Ryder and the Wheels spent their offstage time in a hot, sweaty kitchen—not allowed to mingle with the crowd, too cold to prowl the unfamiliar Village. By summer, the band had learned to take the time between sets to visit the nearby bars, catch a song or two, and get back in time for the next set.

At capacity, about two hundred souls could gather in Trude Heller's. The crowd was a strange mix. Village regulars made room on weekend nights for what Ryder called "the foreigners from New Jersey." Tourists really, "Coming in to see what they considered the freaks." The Village, as with Times Square, offered voyeuristic attractions to what passes for suburbanites in New York (those from New Jersey, Connecticut, and Long Island), rubbing elbows with the night people, who wore long-brimmed hats over faces grown pale for lack of daylight.

"We had ringside seats," said Ryder, who enjoyed being in what he considered the audience to the spectacle that was New York—the man on stage watching the show of the crowd. "We got to look at all this. It was hard to keep our minds on the music, just watching the parade go by."

The Wheels were professional, though, and did indeed pay attention to the sounds they produced. There were others in the New York audience, older men for whom the staff took extra care and prepared tables with white cloths. Record company executives regularly made the rounds of the Village clubs, "artist and repertoire" managers looking for talent.

"You always knew when someone important was coming," Ryder said. "They never told us who, but when the linen came out, you knew something big was going to happen."

Night in, night out, a rotating crew of groups made the rounds of Village clubs, playing through the smoke and noise in hopes of catching the right ear at the right moment. Ryder learned to focus on the show, the song. It would have been easy to get lost in the fog that was a Village bar, both figuratively and otherwise.

"The deeper you went into the Village, especially in the folk sections, the smoke took on a different aroma than normal," Ryder said with a laugh.

Drugs weren't something that New York introduced to the Wheels; they had seen the emerging culture in their own Village, the club in Detroit. Among his first introductions to marijuana came when a member of the Peps asked Ryder if he wanted any "boo." (The explanation of the name, when Ryder asked: "Because if you smoke it, it scares you.")

New York, typical of its nature, took all matters to extremes, both in quantity and brazenness. Anything was fair game; everything was out in the open. "There were many times our eyes bugged out at what we saw in New York," Ryder said. "Even with what I considered my urbane, sophisticated knowledge, I was quite shocked at some of the things I saw."

While in search of their own sound, Ryder and the Wheels continued a musical education that went deep into the roots of rock. They often played with veteran jazz and blues musicians, the previous generation's craftsmen who fathered rock and roll. After establishing themselves at Trude Heller's, the band was put on the road and onstage at other New York venues. In Times Square they played the same bill at the Metropole with legends Gene Kruppa and Dizzy Gillespie. The Wheels alternated sets with Ryder and served as support for the headliner.

One evening at Basin Street East, a memorable name entered the club, trailed by backup singers and carrying a fur-covered guitar. The Wheels were again enlisted as a backup group.

"They were playing behind Bo Diddley," Ryder said. There was down time between sets for Ryder, who asked the management if there was anything he could do to help. "They wanted me to see after Bo's needs," Ryder continued, including the guitarists' demand that a plate of barbecue ribs be ready the minute he finished a set. Ryder made sure the meal was delivered on time.

"What seared into my brain was, after he'd eat the ribs and it was time to go back on, he wouldn't wipe his hands," Ryder said. "He'd just walk up to the stage and grab his guitar. The neck and strings were all covered with barbecue sauce."

The Wheels were respectful to the established stars, voluntarily or otherwise. They were told it was a requirement that the veteran musician be shown certain courtesies. "I had to address him as, 'Mr. Diddley,'" Ryder said. "That sounded so weird. It was like a cartoon name: 'Mr. Diddley.'"

Before long, the Wheels weren't alone in their strange new world, nor was their employment limited to Manhattan. The highways heading north from the city took them to hundreds of clubs to be played, and a small road crew was assigned to get the band back and forth to one-night stands in the area. It was obviously a tiring schedule, for both musicians and their crew.

"We had a couple of road managers," Ryder said. "This one guy, Vince, took us to a gig in upstate New York. On the way, he'd fallen asleep."

Two cars were needed for musicians and equipment, and Ryder was a passenger in the vehicle trailing Vince's. He watched the lead car veer off the road and drive into a house. From Ryder's safe distance, he saw lumber flying, smoke billowing, and people running to or from other parts of the house. Fortunately the car crashed into the living room, and in the early morning hour the family was safely asleep in other rooms. Asleep, at least until a car crashed into their house.

"So they fired Vince and gave us another manager," Ryder said of the obvious outcome.

It was an amateur lapse in an otherwise professional operation. Before spring gave way to summer, Ryder and the Wheels were juggling performance jobs with recording tracks for what would eventually be their first album, and they had learned how to make New York audiences react as strongly as the Detroit teen crowds.

The band had come a long way and was ready to play in the big leagues. Ryder had made all of the requisite first attempts, from singing in church to winning school competitions to making those early recordings in Detroit. The stakes were higher, as were the potential rewards.

The first single recorded in New York, "I Need Help," was a Crewe-penned number Ryder called, "a very good rhythm and blues song," although there were factors going against it becoming a success. The release in August 1965 wasn't the only "Help"-titled song vying for chart space. All things considered, it wasn't much of a contest.

"It came out at the same time the Beatles put out "Help!" Ryder said. "My producer was pretty pissed off. It was a very nicely recorded single, but it didn't sell for shit."

Technically, according to Badanjek, the recording wasn't a true Detroit Wheels effort, as Crewe's separation of singer and musicians was understood to be the unofficial policy from day one.

"Bob Crewe was really interested in Mitch," Badanjek said. "He took Mitch and Jimmy McCarty into the studio with New York studio musicians to record 'I Need Help.' The song went absolutely nowhere. We were all really miffed."

Crewe and the Wheels became all the more determined. Among their next recordings was a frantic rocker using the Wheels' stage technique of combining melodies: two songs for the price of one, really.

It was time for the Wheels to take a ride.

The separation between singer and band had been initiated by Crewe and became evident within a few months of their New York arrival. The group concept, with a name indicating the Star and the Back-Ups (the sort found in plentiful supply among early rock-and-roll bands and the British Invasion, such as Freddie and the Dreamers or Paul Revere and the Raiders), was one avenue toward success. Had there been a strong, unified agreement in the direction of the music, that might have been the path chosen by the Wheels.

Crewe, however, also envisioned a solo Ryder career, having had considerable success producing Frankie Valli, who was likewise carving a solo career apart from the Four Seasons. "I Need Help" was effectively a solo record for Ryder, with McCarty the only Wheel on the single.

Recording sessions were divided: Ryder as a lone act and the Wheels as a group. They may have traveled to New York together, but it wasn't too long before the Wheels and Ryder took different routes. Ryder became a frequent dinner guest at what he called Crewe's "little mansion," the producer's spacious quarters in the famed Dakota building on Central

Park West. Ryder was given a look at how the other half lived, both for contrast and excess, notably seen in what might have been considered animal abuse.

In certain circles of Manhattan society, it was popular that year to own a jaguarundi, an exotic breed of cat imported from South America. Crewe added the animal to a menagerie that included a pair of Siamese cats, sleek yet much smaller than the jaguarundi.

"He made the mistake of putting the raw meat for the jaguarundi down on the floor," Ryder said. "We're sitting in the living room, and for about three minutes we heard the most horrifying shrieking and screams." The territorial jaguarundi came upon the Siamese cats and protected the food with a vengeance, all but disemboweling the smaller animals.

It was the ignorance of the excess that disturbed Ryder. "He didn't know that a jaguarundi would kill the Siamese cats, but it was chic to have a jaguarundi so you could tell your friends."

Ryder saw the opulent decadence that was Manhattan at its most glamorous—complete with kangaroo-skin pillows in the living room—and at evening's end returned to the hotel. "I'd go back to the little roach-infested, two fucking rooms we were living in and just dream about that," Ryder said. "I didn't know if I wanted that, but it was so fantastic, so opulent. I'd been in rich houses, but I'd never seen such flamboyant, over-the-top excess."

When they weren't recording, Ryder was invited to watch other artists at work, including early summer sessions that were being held by Bob Dylan, finishing work on an album to be called *Highway 61 Revisited*. Ryder was at Crewe's penthouse apartment when the phone call came, asking if the singer wanted to join an informal group watching the recording sessions. Someone will come by to pick you up, he was told.

Downstairs at the Dakota, Ryder stood on the sidewalk until, twenty minutes later, a Harley-Davidson motorcycle roared up to the curb. "Mitch Ryder, right?" the cyclist confirmed. "Hop on." Off they went, down the concrete canyons of the Upper West Side, en route to the CBS studio on 63rd Street.

"It's so great to hear that famous Harley muffler bouncing off the buildings," Ryder said of the journey. With casual ease, the driver delivered his passenger to the studio, where Ryder watched musical history being made. Ryder was impressed by the invitation, yet curious. He understood folk music, but the tracks he heard being perfected were hardly the three-minute, danceable pop singles that had been the industry standard just one year earlier.

"Dylan broke that mold with 'Like a Rolling Stone,'" Ryder said. The possibilities of a single, even an album, were being stretched by a class of students eager to push the boundaries of their teachers. The Beatles were shedding their cute, mop-top image, and older teenagers and college students sought more substantial music. Rock and roll was growing up right along with the kids. "For the first time, the audience could read—and think," Ryder said.

Guests came and went for the landmark recording sessions, including folk stars Peter, Paul, and Mary, who had successfully recorded Dylan's "Blowin' in the Wind" and other protest anthems. Ryder was proud to be there, but struggled with self-doubts.

"I don't know what he thought of me or why I was there," Ryder said. "My self-esteem had not ripened yet. I thought: I'm not a genius with words. What the fuck am I doing there?"

He was, whether or not it was consciously known, on the fast track to becoming a star. The first hill of the roller coaster was about to be crested.

For their early recording efforts, Ryder and the Wheels wanted to play to the band's strengths, to capture the energy that had proven successful on stage. Both singer and musicians benefited from the education gained on the road as, now, a legitimate Top Ten group. Ryder's vocals and performance before larger and larger audiences was tested on a near-daily basis. On tour the Wheels played behind stars including Chuck Berry, who knew a thing or two about stage energy.

"We were just killing people at our live performances," Ryder said. Crewe booked studio time to record as much of the band's stage repertoire as possible, insurance for when a single succeeded and the market would welcome a full album from the band.

"We went back and forth between doing songs with the group and trying to establish that solo career doing rhythm and blues," Ryder said. A reputation was growing on that front. At the Bell studios, Ryder's recording of "Taking All I Can Get" was heard by Aretha Franklin, who considered making her own version of the song.

Ryder and the Wheels took the best elements of their show and put them to work in the studio. There were a few combinations of melodies that they particularly enjoyed doing onstage, where portions of two songs were merged into an alternating jam.

"We'd get so worked up, we didn't want to stop playing," Ryder said. "It was too much trouble to stop and start all over again, so we would run these songs together."

Crewe liked the idea and helped select two songs bound together as a pair for the group to record. By late summer, an arrangement had been perfected. The Detroit Wheels probably weren't the first group to link a pair of songs, but they may have done it best when they joined Chuck Willis's "C. C. Rider" with Little Richard's "Jenny, Jenny."

The result impressed everyone, including a couple of studio guests. Crewe had recently acquired the North American distribution rights to the Rolling Stones' growing body of work, and visitors to the sessions at the Seventh Avenue Stea-Philips studio included Keith Richards and Brian Jones. Reportedly, Crewe balked at releasing "Jenny Take a Ride" as a single but was talked into it by the Stones guitarists. They recognized a hit when they heard one. So did the record buyers of America.

"The timing for 'Jenny' was perfect," Ryder said, an observation not likely shared by the Animals, who hit the market in December with a single called "See See Rider." Compensation, perhaps, from the music gods for the Wheels' previous misfortune with "I Need Help," both "Jenny" and "C. C. Rider" would be identified as Mitch Ryder songs.

"Eric Burden had a different opinion," Ryder observed. "We beat him by a few weeks. When he did the album version, there's a drum break and you can hear him say, 'Jenny take a ride,' a dig at our hit. He was pissed, but a friendly relationship grew out of it."

"Jenny" had tough competition: Heading into Christmas 1965, a now-classic Top Ten included songs from the Supremes, Simon and Garfunkel, the Byrds, and the aggressive Rolling Stones warning, "Get Off My Cloud."

Music was becoming a world of changing values, a reflection of the challenges facing a nation and a culture. Newspapers that November asked how the Kennedy family was faring two years after the assassination of a president; a young boxer named Clay (referred to in Associated Press style as a "Negro") was taking on Floyd Patterson; and concerns were published claiming, "Marijuana menace grows on campus."

A growing number of Americans were asking more substantial questions. A late November rally in Washington was staged by what the *Detroit Free Press* called, "New Leftists." Led by eighty-one-year-old U.S. Socialist Party leader Norman Thomas, the rally protested what he called, "an immoral and stupid war." Vietnam was becoming a household name after more than 1,500 U.S. military personnel were reported killed since troops had first been sent to Southeast Asia in 1961.

The Wheels weren't kids anymore. Three members of the band were old enough to be drafted into the armed forces: Ryder, bass player Earl Elliott, and guitarist Joe Kubert.

Ryder was the least eligible of the three. His wife and an expected first child made him a low-priority candidate for selective service, although he was sent a draft notice. Letters were written, documents provided, and his number wasn't called. ("I've always thanked my kids for keeping me out of that war," Ryder said.)

The war in Vietnam did change the lineup of the Wheels, though, both for the short-term and against some long-term considerations.

"Earl didn't want to be drafted into the Army," Ryder said, "so he joined the Marines." It was an admirable (if illogical) decision, made by the musician who enjoyed sprinkling his bed sheets with baby powder and wearing a silk glove to avoid guitar-string blisters.

After his discharge, Elliott took a different career path from his fellow musicians. "When he came out, he immediately opened up a gay club," Ryder said. "I was just wondering what the hell goes on in the Marines."

Guitarist Kubert sought an unfortunate method of avoiding military service. "He had heard that, if you had needle tracks, you would not get taken," Ryder said. "So he started shooting up." Kubert was excused from the draft and would soon leave the band. "After they didn't take him, he continued to do drugs, and it ended up killing him."

Kubert passed away in 1991 from liver complications after battling addictions since 1966, the year the Wheels hit the Top Ten national sales charts.

As 1965 drew to a close, the success of "Jenny" called for the band's first album, *Take a Ride*. A group photo placed the five Detroit teenagers amidst a loading-dock's worth of oil drums, playing to the obvious imagery of their Motor City roots.

The holidays allowed for a homecoming. Ryder gladly returned to the apartment he shared with his pregnant wife. It felt like home, like a normal life, although it was obvious that some things had changed.

"I remember the radio alarm came on, and there it was: 'Jenny Take a Ride.' The disc jockey said something like, 'If that doesn't wake you up, nothing will,'" Ryder said.

Not the typical start to a day back home. Reading the morning paper, Ryder saw that the *Detroit Free Press* listed "Jenny" near the top of the local singles' chart.

"I couldn't believe that feeling," Ryder said. He'd heard a song of his on the radio before, but that experience was clouded with the memory of money exchanging hands. This was a hot, happening sound that blared across southeast Michigan from AM stations CKLW and WKNR. "I was a star. We drove around in a little four-door Corvair convertible, top down, blasting out my song."

Offstage, the question remained if there would be a group or a solo singer supported by backup musicians. The seeds for dissolving the band had been planted by Crewe even before the boys left Detroit, inspiring the advice from Ryder's mother that, no matter what, he keep his own identity.

Ryder knew that a group had a leader. Even the bands that didn't highlight an individual by name were understood to be under the direction of a guiding force. Ray Davies was the man behind the Kinks; Pete Townsend's songwriting gave the Who its identity; and Mick Jagger was obviously more than just the front man while onstage with the Rolling Stones.

"Even though the group concept became big, there always surfaced a leader," Ryder said. "I started as a solo artist, and I wasn't willing to abandon what I had sacrificed to get that."

Hindsight is 20/20, just as predictions can be laughably flawed, even those made by qualified experts. Expectations of the business one year might become outdated within months, and it was impossible to tell who among the explosion of new talent would go the distance with their careers.

In December, *American Bandstand* impresario Dick Clark evaluated the music scene for syndicated columnist Earl Wilson. Among his projections: the merging of folk and rock music wouldn't last; the Dave Clark Five were slipping; and the Rolling Stones had already peaked and would soon disappear.

Others disagreed, including Wilson, who noted that "Get Off My Cloud" was performing well on the charts, and the Stones were excited about their next single, a song opened by a harsh guitar lick called "Satisfaction." Clark's prediction that the pop scene had little use for folk-oriented music was challenged by the year-ending No. 1 single, "Sounds of Silence," which replaced the Byrds' rehashing of the book of Ecclesiastes in "Turn, Turn, Turn." (To his credit, though, America's Oldest Teenager was right about the Dave Clark Five.)

In the second half of the Sixties, there was room on the charts for both folk and philosophy, for rock and roll at full volume, ambitious arrangements featuring orchestral instruments, and even a rhythm and blues singer from the Midwest.

"Jenny" made a December debut on local charts compiled by Detroit radio stations, including old friend Bob Greene from WKNR, Walled Lake Casino host Lee Alan, and Tom Greene at the area's top pop station (broadcast from Windsor, Ontario), CKLW ("The Motor Cit-eee," as sung in the station's signature jingle).

By New Year's Eve, "Jenny" was the No. 1 song in Detroit and ready to take a place on the national Top Ten. The thrill of the record came with an equal concern in an industry that constantly asks, "What's next?"

"We'd been around enough to hear the one-hit wonders," Ryder said. "We became aware of the fact that we had to repeat that success. Like Adam said to Eve: 'Stand back, I don't know how big this is going to get.'"

CHAPTER FOUR

GOOD GOLLY

The success of "Jenny Take a Ride" didn't make Mitch Ryder a rich man, although people assumed that wealth immediately followed celebrity.

"The perception was that I was rolling in dough," Ryder said. "But there wasn't that much money. I just thought it was great to be able to afford my own place, even if it was an apartment."

He was a hometown hero, though. Detroit was proud of Ryder, quick to lay claim to the talent that rises from its streets. The local papers eagerly and often made mention of the newest star, and "coming home" included as much work as it did opportunities to relax with his family, precious time squeezed in between personal appearances, photo sessions, and newspaper interviews. There were odd moments to be enjoyed: seeing his picture in the *Detroit Free Press* or cruising the familiar streets while listening to his own hit record on the radio.

Ryder had reason to celebrate. Invitations to the Top Ten seemed limited to those positions not occupied by the Beatles, whose *Rubber Soul* album that year contained enough hit singles to sustain most lifelong careers. Chart positions were held by a diverse lineup of classic talent, from Simon and Garfunkel to Brian Wilson's arrangements and, closer to home, the factory that was Motown. A year earlier, Ryder had been a fan; he was now a contemporary.

Life doesn't change overnight, and a carefree morning spent cruising the streets to his own soundtrack was a rare moment of abandon. "What came more rapidly was the recognition," Ryder said. Money may not have poured in (although one early indulgence was to finally trade in Ryder's four-door Corvair for an Oldsmobile Toronado), but the perception of celebrity carried more than its weight in gold. When he wasn't appearing before crowds of fans, Ryder tried to accept both fame and fatherhood while barely into his own adult years. He took the family on the road whenever possible and had them visit New York during rare weekends that didn't include travel or performances. The anticipated money seemed impressive but hardly equal to the task of relocating to New York.

"We looked at some apartments on the Upper East Side," Ryder said. "My God, they wanted so much money. We could have made twelve mortgage payments for what it cost to live a month in Manhattan."

To keep the singer happy, producer and manager Bob Crewe arranged a $15,000 down payment for a small home in Southfield. Ryder used the limited negotiating skills he had acquired by that point. "I told Bob that I wanted this house," Ryder said, "and that if I didn't get it, I was going to be very sad and very pissed off."

The $15,000 was the bulk of the limited money Ryder received that year, other than a small cut of ticket receipts. It seemed, however, that there should have been more income. The difference between being a promising act and a band with a Top Ten record invited delusions of grander wealth.

"Before our first hit record, we were working at a club in upstate New York," Ryder said, grueling work, for the band and singer. "Five frigging sets a night, six days a week," for a total compensation of about $1,500 (divided by five, minus expenses).

Then "Jenny" made the charts. Phone calls were made, and the same

$1,500 was being offered for a brief appearance as a featured act in Pittsburgh.

"That was our new reality," Ryder said. "Getting the same money for ten minutes' work." He was traveling the fast lane to fame, a trip that demanded both holding what had been achieved and pursuing more.

Celebration of a hit record lasts about as long as it takes to ask, "What's next?" There was money to be made, as proven by the Beach Boys and a flurry of English acts trying to ride an accented road to fortune. The unspoken fear that came with having a record make it to the Top Ten was that it would also be a group's swan song.

"There were all these one-hit wonders coming out of England that were not getting big money, because they only had one hit," Ryder said.

In March, with the release of "Little Latin Lupe Lu," Ryder was able to breathe a little easier when the song was certified as a hit single.

"The second hit established us as a sound, a certain voice to be recognized," Ryder said. "It removed the one-hit-wonder mantle from our back, and everybody in the industry realized there's some potential here. We just don't know exactly what."

The modest accommodations at the Coliseum House were no longer sufficient for names heard on hit records, faces seen on television. Mitch Ryder and the Detroit Wheels were moving up—and apart. It was clear that Ryder was the star and the Wheels were of secondary concern to Crewe. When they weren't needed, what was left of the original group went back to Detroit while their singer was trained for celebrity.

"The band was sent home," Ryder said. "I stayed in New York to do photo shoots, interviews, the pilot vocals on tracks." When Ryder wasn't being treated like a star or working in the studio, he attended a seemingly endless series of meetings with publishers and writers and was given dance lessons and other instructions.

"I was sent to acting school, and to some fucking lady who would teach me how to eat and which silverware to use," Ryder said. "The grooming process began."

Given a choice, Ryder would have preferred to keep doing what he was doing: knocking out audiences with a high-energy stage show and spending time with the talented musicians of New York's club scene. "I was kind of bitter about it," Ryder said. "The band was allowed to go home. I had to stay and learn all that shit."

Behind every good-time party band is a business, and Mitch Ryder was now, officially, a commodity. Crewe—busy with his own recordings and the Four Seasons—was no longer able to manage the day-to-day business affairs of a legitimate rising star. Manager Alan Stroh (no relation to the Detroit beer family) was assigned the task of turning a Top Ten hit into a career.

"After the hit, we had a meeting where we had to get an agent," Ryder said. Stroh was a more comfortable companion for Ryder's idea of a singing career than Crewe had been.

"Alan had a better vision of what was going on around the music industry than Bob did," Ryder said. "He saw what I was trying to do and agreed with me about the marketplace."

Mitch Ryder and the Detroit Wheels signed a contract with Frank Barcelona and Premiere Talent, a notable agency responsible for the American affairs of top British acts including the Who. In the early months of 1966—riding on the strength of a Top Ten hit with "Jenny"—Stroh was turning Ryder into a music star while Crewe tried to mold him into an all-purpose celebrity.

At first, Ryder was a guest in Crewe's spacious apartment ("little fucking mansion," in Ryder's words) in the Dakota building, where film stars and diplomats were as common a sight as the doorman wearing a crisp uniform. Later, when Crewe took over a Fifth Avenue triplex previously owned by Tony Bennett, Ryder recognized the level of players in the game he was joining.

Crewe's flair for the lavish life (seen through Ryder's twenty-year-old eyes as "the real hoity-toity lifestyle") included dreams of transforming Ryder into the complete pop star. He was sent on arranged "dates" by Crewe, more to be seen than to become romantically involved, with companions such as Liza Minnelli. Crewe's world favored theatrical rather than music stars, and penthouse guests included actor Sal Mineo, with whom Ryder shared a distaste for the direction of one party held at Crewe's.

"Sal and I were at the Dakota one evening. There was a group orgy going on," Ryder remembered. "It was insane, like thirty people groping on a bed. Just, very bizarre. Neither of us wanted to be involved in that, and we hit upon the idea to go somewhere, find a club, just get away from that."

Separately, Ryder was broadening his circle of encounters from the music world. Clubs may officially close at a certain hour of the morning, but parties can still be easily found. Ryder's nightclub hopping could keep pace with that of most other musicians, although he remembered Keith Richards won that undeclared contest one night.

An interesting crowd, and with a hit record, Ryder was now one of them.

"I never had to pay for anything," Ryder laughed. "What's funny to me about the situation, we had a jam session where I played drums, Otis Redding sang, Neil Young played bass, and Stephen Stills played guitar. The only ones in the audience were Brian Jones and his two girlfriends."

In hindsight, a most impressive all-star band, and one would assume that the new rock royalty would have certain airs about their position. Mostly they just wanted to play.

"None of us really took it serious," Ryder said. "People were saying you're so lucky or talented or whatever. We just wanted to have some fun with it. We didn't believe any of this was for real."

Roaming his native Detroit streets while his own hit record blared from the dashboard (in the days when music came from a sole speaker wedged under the windshield) was a random moment of abandon, but the quirks and perks of celebrity were rare occasions during a whirlwind of activity. There was always work to be done, places to be.

"Your schedule gets so hectic," Ryder said. "When you're not on the road you're recording, or doing interviews, doing shows. Every minute of your time is spoken for."

Historically that seems to be the test. One-hit wonders don't disappear due to a lack of talent. Staying in the profession, having success are not based just on artistic ability. "Once you arrive at fame's doorstep, you become its servant," Ryder said. "It doesn't serve you anymore; you become its servant. It's very demanding."

In many ways, Ryder was alone against those demands. Crewe did not consider the Detroit Wheels to be an equal partnership—or a team dominated by two or three key players in the manner of the Beatles, the Who, or the Beach Boys. Still, Ryder and the Wheels tried pushing the doors of celebrity perks open wide enough to fit the entire group whenever possible.

"We did stupid things," Ryder said. "Chrysler wanted to use our name to represent automobiles." The deal was never realized, given the limited offer of one gratis vehicle to be given to the Detroit Wheels.

"They only wanted to give us one. We wanted five," Ryder said, laughing at the brazen response by young men. "It was punk thinking, but we figured if they could afford to give us one, they could afford to give us five."

There were occasional perks. A drum manufacturer wanted to have Badanjek's endorsement on a product line, and five drum kits were offered to the group. "We had the, 'Give to one, give to all' mentality," Ryder said of the demand. "I'm not a drummer, but I ended up with a set of drums. That's one of the upsides—the swag."

For every perk, becoming a famous person in America offered Ryder a balancing loss. He was kept too busy to understand fully the price being paid. There were occasional moments, time to reflect when a twenty-year-old Ryder found an hour alone for a quiet walk in Central Park. He had plenty of questions, but he was unable to come up with even a hint of the answers. On those infrequent walks, he tried to put his journey into some form of perspective, but just as quickly he was back in the tornado of fame.

On a rare vacation, a long weekend in the Bahamas, Ryder was approached by someone more interested in the business end of entertainment than the sounds being played. "Some New York guy who had a few hamburger stands on Long Island called Big Daddy's had the nerve to approach me," Ryder said. An invitation was extended, and repeated with determination, that Ryder should visit a Big Daddy's and meet some fans.

"Just to get rid of him, I said okay," Ryder said. "When I got back to New York, I got a call from Big Daddy. I had to hire a limo to go out to his hamburger stand, and there were maybe sixteen screaming girls waiting."

Complaints from the star fell on deaf ears. Ryder was "lucky," he was told time and time again by Crewe, record company executives, and others. "'Not everybody gets to be a star, and you need to do what you're told,'" Ryder was advised.

"It wasn't a real world anymore," Ryder said. "I was being handled from place to place, told I needed to do that because I was lucky."

Mostly Ryder just wanted to sing, preferably rhythm and blues, the music that first attracted him to the business. He began to wonder if the business would threaten the attractiveness of the music.

"That naïve purpose would soon be squashed," he said. "That's where the danger hits. If I ever had control, it would surely be taken away from me. All I would have to reclaim was whatever natural talents I brought to the table."

When Ryder was a teenager, he was inspired by the acts he saw perform on stage. The circle of life dictated that some members of his audience would in turn be impressed by the show and realize their own life's calling.

In the case of Chrissie Hynde—the voice and guitar talent of the Pretenders—the theatrics onstage were as inspiring as the music being played. "I went to see Mitch Ryder and the Detroit Wheels at an amusement park when I was thirteen," Hynde told the *San Diego Union-Tribune* in 2006. "They had a fistfight onstage. I was mesmerized! I begged some friends to stay and watch the second show with me. They had the same fistfight again. That's when I began to realize what showbiz is all about."

The show that a young Hynde saw was in her native Ohio and provided a memorable night. For Ryder it was just another stop in the whirlwind touring schedule to capitalize on "Jenny." Ryder remembered the stage fight as an impromptu bit of theater prompted by an actual argument. Ryder doesn't remember what started the fight but easily recalled the response it generated: excitement from the audience.

"We were on break and said, 'That went over pretty good.' You're just thinking, whatever the fuck works. If corn started dropping from the sky and people applauded, we'd find a way to make corn drop from the sky."

Ryder knew they weren't inventing anything. The Kinks (already predisposed toward inner-group tensions with two brothers in their own band) had been known to get a little rowdy on stage, and a new band that year from England called the Who was incapable of just standing on stage and performing a song; twirling microphones or flying drumsticks were occasionally aimed at other members of the band.

The audience loved it, and rock-and-roll stars strongly adhered to the P. T. Barnum philosophy of giving the audience what was expected: Shocking onstage theatrics were just part of the game. All bets were off in this new world of pop music, which was as hard to define as it was to categorize.

Ryder participated in a handful of tours billed as the Dick Clark Caravan of Stars. For the teenager in Middle America, the collection of acts reflected the inventory of 45-rpm records spun on monophonic turntables, played beneath bedroom posters of favored musicians.

"Having a Top Ten record within two or three months was part of the criteria," Ryder said. "We did three or four of those, bus rides from city to city. You'd have a girl group—who promised their mothers that a man would never touch them—on a bus with savages who can only think of getting laid. Then you had the peacemakers who were probably gay. It was a circus."

It was a portable hit parade; a half dozen or so acts spending endless hours riding monotonous highways in order to fulfill a ticket holder's fantasy night. A dozen or more cities would be visited, each act playing ten minutes ("fifteen if you were lucky," Ryder said), unleashing their song in front of a screaming crowd before getting back on the bus and heading for the next town.

The diversity of talent and the range of musical styles did not go unappreciated by the artists themselves. Girl groups, early pioneers of what would be called punk rock, folk artists, and young guitar gods rolled together across the highways, savoring their ten minutes onstage and enjoying the other acts. Uncertain what to do with this rising cash cow of talent, promoters were unable to place too many limits on behavior, either onstage or offstage. "To watch the show was even more bizarre," Ryder said. "We never stopped watching the show. We were spellbound. What fucking mad scientist put this thing together? Who are we appealing to?"

Sometimes the music attracted crowds that shouldn't mix with one another. Not every story was amusing in its innocence, and chances at stardom included a selection process. "People who caused problems on the road were immediately removed from the tour," Ryder said. Members of one forgotten group included, Ryder said, "this one drunken asshole" who took advantage of the situation.

"This girl had come by. She wanted to be near fame," Ryder recalled with a sigh. The teenage fan borrowed her father's car to see the show, which was destroyed when the "drunken asshole" took it for a joy ride.

"He ended up burning the engine out, destroying the car," Ryder said. Among other things. The girl was taken back to the hotel room, where she was told she would be at the service of the band. It was, he said, a gang rape that could so easily have been avoided.

The idea of what would be called "groupies"—a new name for an old hobby—was abstract to Ryder, especially when it escalated according to the popularity of three minutes' worth of music.

"In high school, I was a loner, not an attractive person, wasn't really popular with the girls," Ryder said. "After fame came, the most beautiful girls in the world were lining up to give me everything they could. They were, literally, knocking on my door wanting to go to bed. I had to rub my eyes: What weird dream is this?"

Package tours such as the Dick Clark outings played to arenas or wherever the growing crowds could fit; amusement parks and state fairs were traditional rock-and-roll venues. ("Elvis used to do those from flatbed trucks," Ryder said.) Universities were becoming lucrative, reflecting the status popular music was gaining beyond high school. The former sock-hop audience was growing up and wanted their music to do the same.

Establishing a sound with "Jenny" (and, in March, "Latin Lupe Lu"), Ryder played the game according to the formula that Crewe knew worked. If New York had stunned Ryder's senses, the nonstop montage of city "Welcome" signs expanded the twenty-year-old's perception of the country. After leaving a small upstate New York club for a toast-of-the-town venue in Pittsburgh to promote "Jenny," Ryder—with or without the Caravan of Stars—was given a crash course in American geography. Chicago, San Francisco, Dallas, and Philadelphia were home to audiences who understood Ryder's music. Away from the initial comfort zones of Detroit and New York, Ryder learned how big a country the United States was, seen in a series of one-day stops squeezed in between recording dates, photo sessions, and press interviews.

"There are very important impressions the first time you see a city, even Hartford, Connecticut," Ryder said. "Or Atlanta, Miami, New Orleans, Houston. I went across the entire map."

Ryder and one set of Wheels or another became part of a whirling scene of concerts and television appearances, sought after both for the hits they produced and the records they could be expected to make.

"As long as the hits kept coming we were in hot demand," said drummer Badanjek, who—along with guitarist McCarty—represented what was left of the original Detroit Wheels. Television shows ranging from Clark's *American Bandstand* to its seeming legion of imitators including *Shindig, Hullabaloo,* and *Where the Action Is* joined a schedule that put the Wheels on the road with Jeff Beck's Yardbirds, Paul Revere and the Raiders, and Jay and the Americans.

Conventional wisdom held that certain sounds and musical origins worked in certain cities but not others. The mongrel roots of rock and roll, by definition, caught diverse ears with its potpourri of influences. It wasn't just rhythm and blues, or jazz, or rock that informed this new sound.

"Listen to the beat on 'C. C. Rider,'" Ryder observed. "The song itself was kind of gospel sounding. I was pleased with the success of the live

A publicity shot for "Too Many Fish" was among the last photos of the original Wheels (*left to right*): Mitch Ryder, Earl Elliott, Joe Kubert, Jim McCarty, and John Badanjek. (Photo from the Robert Matheu Collection.)

thing, an acceptance of the music I wanted to do."

Success has a demanding appetite, however, and there was little time for long-term planning. Invitations to Caravans of Stars or other concert tours required payments that had to be updated on demand.

"God knows," Ryder said, "if you have a hit record, they want a second one. Immediately if they get the second, they want a third, and it goes on until that pony is just dead in the dirt. Ride it down."

Ryder was among the last American generation born into a world where home entertainment was restricted to reading, radio, and family imaginations. In 1950, when Ryder entered kindergarten, less than 10 percent of American households had a television set. Things changed quickly. Six years later, when Elvis Presley was filmed from the waist up on *The Ed Sullivan Show* (which exercised a mild form of censorship that helped the singer earn the "pelvis" nickname), a majority of homes (65 percent) played host to the three existing networks. By 1966, more than 93 percent of American households had television—at least one set per household—as viewing habits began forming a continental drift within the family circle. Television programming offered America a full lineup of talking cars, talking horses, cartoons, and cowboys, clearly favoring younger viewers. The day's popular musicians were more than ready for prime time.

Television, however, may not have been ready for rock and roll. Those who were deemed stars in the early days of TV came from Hollywood screens, Broadway stages, circus acts, and wherever it was that game-show panelists were created. The musical portion of variety shows were typically given to a *Your Hit Parade*-style lineup, with just about anyone singing the day's top songs. If you were destined to be a star in America, you were introduced to audiences via the grainy black-and-white images that flickered (or rolled, if the horizontal hold wasn't properly adjusted) from the living room console, usually positioned to make it convenient for whoever had to get up and change the channel.

Elvis Presley, Chuck Berry, Little Richard, and others may have been included in 1950s TV schedules as novelty acts, but after the 1964 *Sullivan* appearance by the Beatles, both rock stars and TV hosts recognized the need to include this new genre in their regularly scheduled programming. Ed Sullivan, for one, was more than savvy enough to realize which way the musical winds were blowing and became a fast friend to many of the new groups. Sullivan was not above banishing an act "for life," though, as when the Doors made a 1967 appearance in which singer Jim Morrison stubbornly sang the line, "Couldn't get much higher," while performing "Light My Fire." Others among entertainment's old guard weren't as welcoming, as seen in Dean Martin's rolling-eyed smirk while introducing the Rolling Stones for a 1964 appearance.

Ryder was first unleashed on American airwaves with "Jenny," and as the hits kept coming, so did the invitations to play to the cameras. "After the first hit record, we started getting put on stuff like Dick Clark," Ryder said. "We did the obligatory first-hit-record kind of things. Three or four hits down the line, there would be a lot of changes. For example, *American Bandstand* would be in color. I stuck around long enough to qualify for the color version of *Bandstand*.

Just as the NBC peacock unfurled its multihued feathers—seen on most early sets in an assortment of shades that may not have met the sought-after rainbow image—Ryder learned to bring the spontaneity of his stage show to the small screen.

"Art Linkletter had a show, and when I leaped from the top of the set down into the audience, it caused a panic in the studio and viewing audience," Ryder laughed. "People became frightened, didn't know what I was up to. They thought some kind of beast had been unleashed."

They weren't far off in their prediction. Over the next few years, rock-and-roll acts would explode into the American consciousness in a way that radio never dreamed of. (In the case of a 1967 appearance by the Who on *The Smothers Brothers Show,* "explosion" is the literal term for what happened to Keith Moon's drum set at the conclusion of "My Generation.") As the song said: "Rock and roll is here to stay."

It remained a hit-or-miss formula. Ryder appeared on the gamut of talk shows, from Mike Douglas to Merv Griffin to Dick Cavett, with varying results. "They didn't trust rock and roll," Ryder said of many hosts. "Nobody knew what to do with this rock-and-roll beast that decided to shit on the rug."

As often happens, things on television aren't quite as glamorous as they may seem to the viewer. It became a blur to Ryder, who quickly overcame any awe he felt about being in the various television studios so that he could concentrate on the work at hand. Cables underfoot, the studio usually colder than "room temperature," and crews that outnumbered the on-air talent by tenfold or more made for a busy atmosphere. For teenage dance shows such as *American Bandstand* or *Hullabaloo,* Ryder and the Wheels played in a cramped, confined space, flanked by dancers and stalked by cameramen.

The usual practice was for the singer and band to "lip-sync" the performance, pretending to sing while their hit recording was played. (*The Ed Sullivan Show* was one of the few exceptions where bands played live in the studio; on most others, a rehearsal take or two was done live, but the on-air performance was lip-synced.) For Ryder, it was just one more trick to learn about stardom.

Of course, lip-syncing (and, yes, "air guitar") was hardly a novel experience for teenage music fans. Ryder recalled many a time when he did the same thing in his bedroom, practicing in front of a mirror to a James Brown soundtrack.

"That's kid stuff," he said, "pretending to sing a song, looking at yourself in the mirror. When you do it on TV, it's a whole different story. For me, it was a fanatical obsession to get everything perfect."

By its nature, rock and roll or rhythm and blues is a live, spur-of-the-moment performance, but Ryder had to replicate the screams and shouts of the impassioned studio performance of "Jenny." You count beats, Ryder said, learn to twist your neck, deliver the song the way the audience wants it sung.

With the chart success of "Jenny" and "Little Latin Lupe Lu," television appearances were becoming just another day at work, no different than the mini-tours of chart-topping acts that roamed the land to capitalize on hit records. The challenge was not just making the charts, but also in doing it again.

"We needed another hit, that was clear," Ryder said. "It was hard to understand how we were going to get one when we were only doing cover material."

The era of recording other people's songs was coming to an end. It wasn't just the folk singers strumming their protests, á la Dylan, Simon and Garfunkel, or Peter, Paul, and Mary. Rock and roll was giving birth to songwriters beyond the Beatles, Stones, and Beach Boys. Their inspired followers were learning the value of their own material.

Still, cover versions could work: A few months before the March 17, 1966, release of the Wheels' version of "Little Latin Lupe Lu," the Righteous Brothers had modest success with the same song. An identifiable sound was the ticket to long-term success and for the Wheels to continue rolling. Another hit was in order to confirm their identity. Through the summer of 1966, "Breakout" and "Taking All I Can Get" made chart appearances that fell short of the success of "Jenny." For a lasting career, Ryder would have to get back to the hit status of the elite Top Ten ranks.

Long-range plans were hard to imagine for a twenty-year-old who had been invited into the international arm of the "famous" club. Ryder made his first visit that summer to England, where he found an unlikely friend in Lionel Bart, the songwriter responsible for the score of *Oliver!*

"It wasn't a performance tour," Ryder said of his first hop across the pond. Instead, he went to be seen, appearing at the right clubs, being in the company of "the right people," and testing the waters while "Jenny" made a brief run on the British pop charts.

"The most interesting thing to me was staying on good terms with Lionel Bart," Ryder said. "We'd jump into his Rolls-Royce and drive into downtown London." This was during the famous, "swinging London" days, when the old town was trying to celebrate a new sense of freedom while still dimming the automobile headlights at night, a routine left over from the blackout days of World War II.

Some money—not much—was seen that summer, although the growing Levise family settled into their first home. Ryder wasn't often in Detroit, perhaps a week or two at a time, before going back into the world of becoming a star, something that friends, neighbors, and even family began to acknowledge.

"People started to get all excited about the fame," Ryder said. "The neighbor and his wife became very friendly, and a guy from high school—which wasn't that long ago—came trying to sell me an interest in oil wells in Michigan."

By the end of 1966, Ryder would become forever linked to a song, and life would never again be the same.

A keyboard bangs a determined chord, pauses, strikes twice more in rapid succession. Behind this sound, a fluttering foot pedal pounds against a bass drum, a beat that seems to go faster and faster. A scream is heard, one of those definitive, blood-curdling moments clarifying rock and roll. "All right . . . jump up . . . get it," the singer begins, statements of celebration, encouragement, and invitation. The lyrics chant: "Devil with a blue dress, blue dress, blue dress, devil with a blue dress on . . ."

"Ooh, yeah," the singer crows. It felt right, in a way that removes all doubt of what would happen. By the fall of 1966, Ryder and the Wheels were no strangers to the studio, although the recording of "Devil with a Blue Dress On/Good Golly, Miss Molly" included just Ryder, drummer Johnny Badanjek, and guitarist Jimmy McCarty, backed by whatever studio musicians were calling themselves Detroit Wheels that week.

"At that point, we had a bass player we weren't familiar with, a second guitar player, and a keyboard player we weren't familiar with," Ryder said. "We were still Mitch Ryder and the Detroit Wheels, but the Wheels were changing."

The sound was familiar, though, a musical trademark that was both an advantage and possible handicap. As with "Jenny/C. C. Rider," the single paired "Devil with a Blue Dress On" with a Little Richard hit, "Good Golly, Miss Molly." The verses of "Devil" came from an arrangement the band had worked out on stage, covering a regional hit recorded by Shorty Long on Detroit's Soul Label. Ryder and the Wheels had been performing "Devil" as part of their stage arsenal, and didn't require much rehearsal time in the studio. Like the business itself, it was ready to roll, quickly.

Unlike "Jenny," the pairing of "Devil" and "Good Golly, Miss Molly" earned an enthusiastic response from producer Crewe. As the Sixties marched on, Crewe kept his personal party going, even while working in the studio.

"For that recording session—and every session we did with him—it was like going to fucking Carnivale in Rio," Ryder remembered. A shrieking, screaming Crewe jumped on boxes, all over the studio, breathless with the beat, admittedly (in his later years) among the early crowd experimenting with cocaine. "We just wanted to get that song over with so we could get out of there. We were bug-eyed, watching him fly around out of control. We were the only group he did that with; he didn't do that with the Four Seasons."

"Devil" was one of those records that was meant to be, with all the elements of a classic rock single. McCarty pierced the airwaves with a blistering guitar lead played on top of a cascading Badanjek drum roll. Ryder's voice screamed, growled out the infamous phrase: "Good Golly, Miss Molly." They may have been other people's songs originally, but the marriage of the two became identified as the Mitch Ryder sound.

"As it made its way into the Top Ten, there was a recognition factor to the group, and my voice was becoming a distinctive sound," Ryder said.

Others agreed. Beach Boys leader Brian Wilson shook his head during an interview in admiration of, "that voice," no small praise coming from one of rock's premiere vocal arrangers.

"We knew we had something hot," Ryder recalled. The song was a one-day wonder in the studio, recorded live with the first vocal take being the keeper. The two-song mini-medley became the group's trademark sound.

"The formula worked, in a big way," Ryder said. "It established a stereotype of Mitch Ryder and what people could expect: energetic, exciting, frenzied, whatever you want to call it. It established us."

"Devil with a Blue Dress/Good Golly, Miss Molly" was released in October and spent fourteen weeks in the Top Forty. By November 12 it was a Top Ten song, removing any lingering concerns about the "one-hit wonder" label being attached to the group.

The October 15, 1966, issue of *Billboard* magazine, the industry's bible and official scorecard of record sales, profiled Ryder and the Wheels as being among the "Hot 100 Stars" and recognition for "heavy sales and a potential hit record." "Devil" made its debut at No. 59 in a week where Motown's Four Tops lead the pack with, "Reach Out, I'll Be There." A near-classic Top Five that week included the Association's "Cherish," "96 Tears" by ? and the Mysterians (a Saginaw, Michigan–based band), and the Monkees' "Last Train to Clarksville." (The number five position was something called "Psychotic Reaction" by Count Five, a single not destined for nostalgia-laden soundtracks.)

"Devil" peaked in January 1966 at No. 4, keeping respectable company with the Beach Boys' classic "Good Vibrations," and Donovan's semiclassic "Mellow Yellow." (Harder to imagine was competition from the inexplicable No. 1 hit "Winchester Cathedral" by the New Vaudeville Band.)

Throughout the year, Ryder was told he would become a Famous Person and was groomed accordingly. It was the spoils given America's victors of the Chart Wars. With a No. 4 hit featured on best-seller lists for weeks on end, there seemed to be no limit to the future of Mitch Ryder.

"After the first hit, things changed dramatically," Ryder said. "But nowhere near the change after three hits. You're no longer a one-hit wonder; you're an established star. With one hit, it's kind of cool, with the recognition and the fame, but you didn't know how long it was going to last. Typically, not very long. But when you start producing a string of hits, people see you differently."

The business, however, has certain limitations about those it deems a star and those who can become true teen idols. Being a certified Top Ten name offers other opportunities, but the invitation is only for those deemed to have specific qualifications.

"A lot of change came with that record," Ryder said. "The kind of gigs you get, the money, the tours and TV shows you're asked to do." Producer Crewe had hopes that Ryder could become "a pretty boy in those magazines," Ryder said of the dreamboats of the day. He was at his publicist's office and saw the dimpled smile of Bobby Sherman beaming from a glossy magazine cover.

"I said, 'What's he got? Why can't I get on the cover of those stupid teen magazines?'" Ryder asked. The publicist responded, "Quite frankly, Mitch, you're just not pretty enough."

Ryder wasn't destined to become an early pubescent fantasy of teenage girls, but the Mitch Ryder and the Detroit Wheels sound had stronger appeal elsewhere, with an honest rock-and-roll attitude and streetwise heritage of rhythm and blues. The music fan in Ryder could no longer look at other artists with simple, appreciative admiration.

"We understood we had something that we had to work hard to keep," Ryder said. "We saw other groups as competition."

If the singles charts were a contest, Ryder was winning the battles. The singer and the band would either continue engaging in the competition or find other outlets for the energies of young men barely into their twenties.

"If they didn't keep us busy, boredom would set in," Ryder said. "We were young men who were easily distracted."

CHAPTER FIVE

RUNNING WITH THE DEVIL

Even by the quantity-over-quality standards of the day—the object being to flood the market quickly to take advantage of sudden fame—there was enough recorded output during a two-year period for two Mitch Ryders.

In many ways, the singer felt pulled in two directions—between commercial success and artistic achievement—and something had to give.

The breakup of the Detroit Wheels shouldn't have surprised fans, considering the way the group was being presented. Two separate albums were released in early 1967: *All Mitch Ryder Hits* compiled material from the band's two releases the previous year; *Sock It to Me!* offered the third and final Mitch Ryder and the Detroit Wheels LP.

While *Sock It to Me!* featured a batch of new recordings, the goal of *All Mitch Ryder Hits* was, the singer of hits said, pretty obvious. "Repackaging the same old shit."

True enough. The bulk of the compilation's eleven "hits" came from the three existing Mitch Ryder and the Detroit Wheels albums. Fan favorites "Devil with a Blue Dress On" and "Jenny Take a Ride" were included, along with singles released the previous year that hadn't been included on albums.

In addition to the two LPs, producer Bob Crewe maintained a steady flow of singles to keep the market appetite appeased. Studio time was squeezed into an active performing calendar, and Crewe was beginning to experiment, trying to make the Ryder voice more accessible to mainstream, across-the-board audiences. The rough edge of "Devil" and "Jenny" was all well and good, but Crewe had a broader fan base in mind. Singles that followed "Sock It to Me—Baby" (credited to Mitch Ryder and the Detroit Wheels) included a remake of "You Are My Sunshine" and a Motown cover, "Come See about Me." Separately, a single pairing the Big Bopper's "Chantilly Lace" with the standard "Personality" in a Wheelsworthy, two-song blend was released (under the solo credit Mitch Ryder).

The final album credited to the group, *Sock It to Me!* illustrated Crewe's assessment of the band's importance. Big, bold lettering screamed "MITCH RYDER" and "SOCK IT TO ME!" In half-sized letters, "The Detroit Wheels" was sandwiched between the singer and the album title. For those who still didn't understand, the LP's cover illustrated the story: Unlike the group photos on the *Take a Ride* and *Breakout . . . !!!* albums, the front of *Sock It to Me!* was an extreme close up of a screaming Ryder; a picture of the band was on the flip side.

Musically, the album was notable for the title song, "Sock It to Me—Baby," which would eventually sell more copies than "Devil with a Blue Dress On." "Sock It to Me—Baby" was the first song recorded by an all-white group to reach No. 1 on the New York City rhythm-and-blues chart. The phrase was understood in black culture; Aretha Franklin's background choir chanted the verbal riff behind her June 1967 No. 1 hit, "Respect.") However, Ryder was credited with helping to bring it over to mainstream, suburban America. A slogan was launched and used in infamous fashion on the television show *Rowan and Martin's Laugh-In*. The four-word punch line forever lost its street respectability and entered pop culture history in 1968, when presidential candidate Richard M. Nixon appeared on the show and deadpanned a confused delivery of the words: "Sock it to *me*?" His gravelly recitation turned it into a question; all things considered, arguably the most surreal sound bite in the history of television.

Then again, it may have worked: Many attribute part of Nixon's victory over Hubert Humphrey to the Tricky One's willingness to use television, rather than avoid it. Nixon was determined to learn from his Kennedy-debate lesson that, if you wish to win a contemporary election, you'd better look good on TV. (The author would like to note that it would be unfair, at this point in history, to blame Ryder for putting Nixon in the White House.)

In some ways, the album was an ironic swan song. After *Sock It to Me!* the days of the Detroit Wheels were numbered. "For Crewe it was a great awakening," Ryder said. "He had his first hit record without the all-important group. It encouraged his belief that we could attain superstardom without them."

There is no such thing as an overnight success, but, once sparked, fame can quickly blaze to life. In just over two years' time, Ryder's move to New York yielded a handful of hit records, dozens of television appearances and countless concerts before increasingly enthusiastic fans. He was now certifiably a "famous person in America," and there was little time to waste on doubts. Even missed opportunities came and went with casual ease. In January, he was put on standby for a trip to the CBS Television Theater, where Ed Sullivan's weekly potpourri of talent maintained its steady inclusion of rock and roll. Sullivan's people were concerned that Rolling Stones singer Mick Jagger would balk at changing the lyrics to the band's latest hit, "Let's Spend the Night Together," and wanted a backup act ready, just in case.

"He called us the night he threatened the Rolling Stones, so we stood by," Ryder said. The appearance was not meant to be: Jagger accepted the price to be paid and sang a watered-down version of the song, the allegedly innocent-sounding, "Let's spend some time together."

It would have been among the last shows by what was left of the Wheels. The 1967 calendar was a busy one for Ryder, who performed 280 shows with or without the group. Most of the shows were one-nighters: Breeze into town, appear as either a spotlight act or as part of a package tour, and head for the next show somewhere else. Night in, night out, the weeks became months with hardly a break.

"It was just exhausting," Ryder said. "After a while, you're on auto-pilot. You have to trust people to protect you and take care of you, because you're too vulnerable and not strong enough to fend for yourself."

Cities and venues blurred like the shadowy front row of fans, silhouettes behind the footlights. A physical toll was taken. Ryder cancelled one show owing to a throat condition, another time from exhaustion and mononucleosis. Although not part of a band, he belonged to a rotating team of people with specific tasks leading to a shared conclusion.

"The objective of everyone involved is to get you to the gig," Ryder said. "When you're sitting in New York, you have time to be seen or go to parties. But on these large, arduous moneymaking road tours, you don't get any time except time to survive and get to the next gig. That's everybody's agenda: Keep drugs away from him; keep drinks away from him; keep girls away from him; and get him some sleep."

Ryder encountered every cliché imagined about the rock star on tour, with doctors prescribing pills for waking up and prescriptions for the end of the day. "The hours are so fucked up," he said. "If you've only got five hours to sleep, you need to be able to sleep right away. Instead of lying there in bed, praying for sleep, watching the hours tick down, the answer is to take a sleeping pill."

Of course, sleeping pills don't fully wear off after five hours, and getting up becomes harder and harder as the days and weeks take their toll. "One time they had to break into my room I was so exhausted I couldn't be awakened. They had to throw some clothes on me and get me to the gig cause we were so late."

It's hard to focus on a journey's end while riding a roller coaster, with daily spins, drops and thrills. There were temptations and more than just the blur of beautiful women passing by the view. The headlining life was an enjoyable star trip, "a dizzying ride of money, fine hotels, expensive clothes," Ryder said. "It was a flurry."

As a business, somebody was making money off Mitch Ryder. With or without the Wheels, Ryder's voice was heard on six "hit" records in less than two years. It was a pie that didn't lack for people wanting a piece. Companies wanted profits, producers wanted product, and the fans (as they always had and always will) wanted a variety of returns for their affection. Some lined up in search of money, access, a connection to fame.

"It happens at some point," Ryder said. "'Sign this for me, do this for me.' It's weird stuff. It was a busy, busy year."

Musically, the Crewe-directed career was more in tune with the hitmakers of the day than the experimental groups beginning to flex their studio muscles. Crewe's tastes—seen clearly in the loftier ballads released under Frankie Valli's name—pushed for Ryder to become more idol than artist. Separating the singer from the band may not have been Crewe's plan from the start, but it clearly was the result.

"At that point, it was all in his hands," Ryder said. No group would have any input into any kind of creativity. "He wasn't fostering or nurturing that."

Jackie Kaufman thought the event would be more about fashion. The K Girls would be the stars, she thought, and the Wild Fashion Show the highlight of the week. Better, she said, than all that time spent on the entertainment that she referred to as "those damn bands."

The groups cursed by the wife of disc jockey Murray (the K) Kaufmann included a couple of new acts—"Direct from England"—called the Who and Cream, the latter featuring an up-and-coming guitar player named Eric Clapton. Other scheduled performances included Jan and Dean, Wilson Pickett, Smokey Robinson (who was unable to attend), and a couple of new folk kids, Simon and Garfunkel. The event was a week's worth of shows at New York's RKO Theater during the Easter 1967 holiday: massive, ongoing, song-and-dance spectacles thrown by one of New York's most aggressive disc jockeys, Murray the K.

The headliner at the top of the marquee was a familiar name under a new billing. The Mitch Ryder Show was the dominant act over an impressive lineup. His appearance allowed for American exposure for the Who and Cream; Ryder's management firm, Premier Talent, was jockeying to represent both American acts and the newest British talent. Renowned agent Frank Barcelona offered Ryder as a headliner, provided the Murray the K shows made room on the poster for the British groups.

"They were such a big agency, they could talk people into promoting the English acts," Ryder said. "They would balance that by taking their proven American stars and working us to death so they could finance the British invasion."

Kaufmann—famous for manipulating his way into the Beatles' inner circle during the boys' first U.S. tour and proclaiming himself "the Fifth Beatle"—was a promoter with grandiose visions somewhere between Ed Sullivan and P. T. Barnum. The concerts were held over nine consecutive days, March 25 to April 2. Making the most of a twenty-four-hour clock, Kaufmann's strategy was to fill the theater five times daily, beginning at 10:15 a.m. and running past midnight.

For the performers, the schedule allowed less than ten minutes per act, barely enough time, said Keith Moon of the Who, to do abbreviated versions of "My Generation" and "Can't Explain," destroy their equipment, and run offstage. Kaufmann encouraged the Who's trademark explosive conclusion—during which Pete Townshend's guitar and Moon's drum kit were smashed with abandon—but asked that it be done with "as little damage as possible."

If the limited time and multiple shows challenged the Who's equipment budget, it dampened the true talent of guitarist Clapton; the days of the three-minute pop single were giving way to compositions best played in extended format, including Cream's "I'm So Glad" and "Spoonful."

"The shows were maybe ten minutes each. I got fifteen because I was the headliner," Ryder said. "You did that five times a day, and the rest of the time you had to just be there. You couldn't wander off after the show."

Backstage, the schedule was perhaps too generous with down time; the idle hours between performances weren't quite long enough for the artists to leave the theater. Boredom wasn't the best friend of Moon, Cream drummer Ginger Baker, and some of the other personalities inhabiting the RKO that week. More seasoned musicians such as Pickett were less than amused at the juvenile flour fights, flooded changing rooms, smoke bombs, and other pranks. "Everybody ended up just hanging around," Ryder said, "desecrating the dressing rooms and causing havoc."

To the audience, the concert was a dream come true, presenting the new direction of "rock and roll," if it could still be called that. Innocent sock-hop fans would blush at the advances of this new music, born of grittier origins. The title proposition of "Sock It to Me, Baby" was hardly subtle in its sexuality; the guitar riff after the key phrase itself sounded obscene. Music included social statements as well as the traditional (albeit heightened) sexuality. The Who voiced a new generation's perception of the one that came before: "Why don't you all . . . f-f-fade away."

The change in music wasn't just the evolution of an art form: Onstage and offstage, the young voices began pushing the limits beyond the composition of a song or the handling of an instrument. They were playing with the nature of celebrity itself, and few embodied that attitude more than the Who's drummer, Keith Moon.

"All the stories I heard about him was that he was absolutely nuts," Ryder said. "Even by our wild standards, he was on the edge." A new animal had been born at the rock-and-roll zoo, one who concluded performances by kicking, pounding, destroying his drum kit. When given the national spotlight on *The Smothers Brothers Comedy Hour*, Moon packed the bass drum with an excessive amount of explosives for a grand finale.

It wasn't all just an act. For Moon, "the show must go on" continued after the show. "His behavior on stage was less offensive than his behavior offstage," Ryder said. "He was very cynical, very sarcastic, and very vocal about his dislikes." Later that year, Ryder hosted the Who when they appeared in Detroit. They went to the Roostertail, where Frank Sinatra Jr. was performing. Moon made no secret of his belief that the second-generation singer was trying to cash in on the father's famous name.

"As Frank Jr. approached the stage, Keith threw a lit cigarette at his feet, called him, 'rubbish,' and walked out," Ryder said. An awkward moment, socially: Ryder was the hometown host in the prominent Detroit club, and the Who were his guests. "I was torn between leaving with the Who and social etiquette," Ryder said. "I stayed."

The social politics of rock stardom may have confused Ryder, but there was no hesitation on his part while commanding the RKO stage during the Murray the K shows. Bruce Conforth, a University of Michigan professor of American Culture and original curator of the Rock and Roll Hall of Fame Museum, was a young musician then living in Greenwich Village. Conforth was among the shuffling crowds that packed the RKO that week and said that Ryder's acceptance by New York's hip youth certified the crossover appeal of black sounds and culture invading white America.

"Had we known that this white guy was singing soul and rhythm and blues, we would have been surprised," Conforth said. "We were surprised when Stevie Winwood came out in the same way. You had all these people coming around supposed to be doing blue-eyed soul, and Mitch was doing it way before they were."

And doing it well. In spite of the impressive lineup of musicians, Conforth recalled a dominant voice. "He was headlining over all this, and I can honestly say he came out and blew people away. When we first heard the stuff Mitch was doing, it was like, 'Wow. Who is this guy?'"

A valid question; in some ways, Ryder himself wasn't sure. Having spent years trying to perfect the rhythm-and-blues song—one that could make an audience stand up, dance, yell, and applaud—Ryder was not as confident backstage as he was singing into a microphone. Each day, five shows a day for a week, Ryder delivered all you could ask from a headliner: Girls screamed, kids rocked, heads and hips swiveled with determination.

When the headliner stepped offstage, another story was emerging. Music had taken on more importance for its audience; the artists were challenged to become more than just musicians. The talent Ryder saw emerging raised the bar, an observation he made while watching Eric Clapton stretch the boundaries of the electric guitar to new levels.

Was it enough to be a singer specializing in rhythm and blues in this new world?

"It scared the shit out of me," Ryder said. "I was sitting to the side of the show, watching Cream. I could see the writing on the wall, the change that had come, and there was no room for me," Ryder said.

Ryder watched the group's young, reserved guitar player. During the week, Clapton found quiet hallway spaces; sitting alone and tuning his instrument, letting his fingers explore the language. The audience may not have fully understood what it was hearing—not quite yet—but the trained musician Ryder heard it loud and clear.

"Eric Clapton single-mindedly believed in himself and knew that he should have been the headliner," Ryder said. "You could sense it about him—the way he stood, the confidence he exuded on stage. He knew that his time, if it hadn't already arrived, would shortly, and there was nothing I could do to change that. It was bigger than just losing my fans; it was about the change in music."

Records were no longer made during brief sessions in the studio—scheduled quickly to meet the instant demand of a pop-buying public. Singers were now songwriters with more to say than just another variation of "Boy Loves Girl," and it wasn't just the "folkies" in the wake of Bob Dylan who were trying to make a statement.

Ryder wondered if what he brought to the table was good enough. "There's nothing too challenging about the words, 'Fee-fee-fi-fi-fo-fo-fum,'" Ryder said, a phrase from "Devil with a Blue Dress On" that he chanted at every show.

Two years earlier, Ryder had been the new kid in town. As inevitable as the tide—accelerated, perhaps—Ryder was now the veteran, looking over his shoulder at the newcomers trying to stake a claim on his territory.

"There's gonna be a gunfight," Ryder said. "It takes a killer to know a killer, and it was a little scary. Not because I minded moving out of the way, but because I didn't know what more I could do, and it scared me."

There are many ways to measure fame: Wealth, power and recognition are the obvious indicators. Artists and producers scrambled to cash in on pop music's now industry-leading appeal.

In America, you've truly made it when someone makes a version of you out of plastic and people buy it. As part of its Show Biz Babies series, the Hasbro Company included a 4 1/4-inch-tall Mitch Ryder, bedecked in a silver lamé jumpsuit and packaged with a floppy 33 1/3-rpm single of "Sock It to Me—Baby." In 1967 and 1968, the company produced dolls bearing the likenesses of the Monkees, the Mamas and the Papas, and individual singers including Bobby Gentry, Peter Noone (of Herman's Hermits), and Mitch Ryder.

Ryder's career was spinning faster than the records he produced. He knew the promotion had been arranged, but he hadn't seen a copy until noticing the Show Biz Babies bin at Kresge's department store. "We bought a few. One for my mom. It was strange. I wasn't impressed with the doll as much as being in the same bin with the Mamas and the Papas and all them. That's what I was impressed with."

With the previous year's hits, 1967 appeared poised to be the year Ryder would take the final step up the ladder of fame. "I was becoming real close to being a superstar, for what it was at that time," he said. "I made the mistake, for a brief time, of believing that it was because of me. In the end, it was because of the amount of money, power or impact your fame might have at that given moment. I didn't realize that could change so quickly and a new guy would be standing in my shoes a day later. It was frustrating."

Ryder yearned to become the featured rhythm-and-blues voice of his generation, while Crewe tried to groom the all-around image immortalized in a collectible toy. Celebrity dolls weren't the only product vying for dollars earned through baby-sitting or newspaper deliveries: Lunch boxes, toy instruments, posters and pillow cases, trading cards and anything anyone could think of gambled on the next 'mania' that might grip American teenagers.

Some experiments, in hindsight, were perhaps ill conceived. Michigan's Shafer Bakeries launched a cross-promotion with Motown head Berry Gordy, who may have lost touch with contemporary slang terms.

"They came out with these tiny loaves of kids' bread with pictures of the Supremes on the wrappers," Ryder laughed. "Supremes White Bread. [Gordy's] understanding of racism in Detroit totally eluded him—people were laughing their asses off. They thought it was going to be like Aunt

Jemima pancakes or something." Gordy and Schafer Bakeries canceled the short-lived promotion while journalists in the black press composed harsh editorial opinions.

Gordy, however, was now head of one of the most successful record companies in the business, without "Detroit" or "black-owned" qualifying that description. He was confident enough to consider recording white artists.

"After I had success, Gordy asked me if I'd like to come over," Ryder said of the invitation to join the Motown family. "It's a little late, isn't it?" Ryder responded.

Mostly, as 1967 rolled along with the hits, Ryder was getting tired. "That was a very difficult year in terms of energy. People look and say, 'Wow, what a great life,' but they have no idea how much work is involved."

Exhausted, torn, divided, and sold, Ryder was in a state of culture shock, exposed to wealth and fame that invited him to the party. "Every door opened for me," he recalled. "I didn't have to ask twice. Coming from a poor background into a lavish life like that is like jumping into Lake Michigan in November to take a swim. It's heavy duty."

Spring gave way to what would be called the Summer of Love, for most people a reality not quite as romantic as the brief claim of spiritual enlightenment. Ryder's ascension to the most hallowed ranks of current fame was certified by a strangely worded, elite invitation; a party was being thrown to celebrate the new Beatles album.

By late May 1967, some pop-culture critics had written the Beatles off. They were yesterday's news, was the claim of these analysts who believed that the ever-present rush to find (and market) the next new thing would send the "older" groups packing.

What those who wanted to dismiss the Beatles didn't know was that the next sound was being prepared and the former Mop Tops were about to change rock music in ways few could imagine.

Critics aside, the stature of the Beatles remained dominant on London's social scene; Ryder was in the audience when the Liverpool lads were guests of honor at the Speakeasy on May 24. Procol Harem performed publicly for the first time their composition "Whiter Shade of Pale," yet another dialect in the changing musical language—a moody, orchestral piece bringing classical organ sounds into the rock arsenal.

"It was a very special night," said Ryder, who was in London for a promotional trip, enjoying the privileges bestowed on singers of hit songs. "The Beatles sat in a cubicle of sorts, all wearing their Sgt. Pepper uniforms. London was pretty wild in those days."

The Beatles album *Sgt. Pepper's Lonely Hearts Club Band* has been credited with, among other things, launching the Summer of Love, inventing the psychedelic movement, and originating what would be called "concept" albums (although Bob Dylan and the Beach Boys had already released comparable "theme" albums by then). One thing was certain: *Sgt. Pepper* was an invitation to explore new paths, music simply being one of them.

Ryder was invited to share in the celebration. Instructions for getting to the party were suitably confusing. "They weren't your typical directions," he said. "They said things like, 'Drive into the sun for twenty or thirty miles.' They weren't very specific."

They neared their destination. They drove to a field, a pasture, and were told to look for "a girl with kaleidoscope eyes," a phrase from the album's song "Lucy in the Sky with Diamonds."

"Damn if we didn't drive out there, and damn if she wasn't there," Ryder said. "Wow! We looked for the next clue, and it all had to do with things out of *Sgt. Pepper*."

Arriving at the house, the country home arranged for by Beatles manager Brian Epstein, was definitely a case of, "You'll know it when you see it."

"We finally get to this farmhouse, and in the driveway was this Rolls-Royce with paisley paint all over it," Ryder said. John Lennon had taken delivery earlier that month of his psychedelic Rolls, among the truest marriages of pop art and commerce of its day.

Three of the four Beatles were in residence (Paul McCartney was in America that week), as were the singer Lulu, Beatle wives, and a host of London's reigning society. The drug habits of a generation were in evidence, including an entry-hall bowl filled with marijuana-hashish mixed joints. At first, Ryder was too blown away by his surroundings to worry about artificial manipulations of reality.

"A lot of people considered me a star, but I stood humbled in the presence of the Beatles. They were our gods," Ryder said. "I was a fan before I became an artist, so when we got to a Beatles party, it was a really, really big deal."

Ryder settled in at the affair, a laid-back gathering of the highest order. He dropped some acid, "to be part of the gang," but felt a lack of confidence. Ryder and his wife took some quiet time in a small room that held little more than a piano. He noodled around with some chords and began playing a song for his wife.

Midway through his serenade, Beatles publicist Derek Taylor entered the room, along with George Harrison. The greeting, Ryder said, was less than pleasant. "Taylor looked at me and said, 'Get the fuck outta here. We wanna use the piano.' No regard for me whatsoever," Ryder said. "I was angry, because he insulted me and my wife, but wasn't sure what to do. I know what I wanted to do to Taylor, but then there was George, the god, standing there. So we withdrew."

Having been snubbed by a Beatle was hard to take: "It put me on this slow spin into bummer-hood," Ryder said. "I had the feeling my brain was expanding, but maybe I mistook the fact that it was going to blow up as an expansion."

Undaunted, the usually genial Ryder spotted Beatles drummer Ringo Starr seated alone at a large table facing a fireplace. "He was looking depressed, sitting in front of a big, walk-in fireplace," Ryder said. "So I went over to him and asked, 'Wanna play some cards?' And he just stared at me. A little smile came out of the corner of his mouth."

Before Starr could answer, a Beatles employee interrupted the conversation, concerned that one of the golden hosts was being upset. Ryder was told to let Ringo have his space (understood to be a private drug journey). "Who are you? You're not happening." The employee backed Ryder off, away from his second Beatle encounter.

"So now I've been rejected by two of the four gods that lived in my world," Ryder laughed. "I had a fifty-fifty chance of staying alive or being assassinated. I was really, really bummed and started having a bad trip." Dejected, rejected, Ryder sank into the end of a lengthy sofa, staring at the largest fireplace he'd ever seen. "That fucking fireplace, you could have a football game in there. I was just sitting there bumming out."

It was a crowded party, and Ryder wasn't able to be alone with his thoughts. He was next targeted by a one-man welcome wagon intent on keeping the mood happy.

"All of a sudden this guy comes along, trying to cheer me up," Ryder said. "He jumped up and down like a clown, danced around, telling me not to be sad." The Samaritan did whatever it took to make sure Ryder enjoyed the party.

"That was John Lennon," Ryder said. "He spent a half hour working on me, being my friend, putting me back in a good frame of mind. He was the only one that cared about somebody other than himself."

Ryder meant more than identification when he said, "That was John Lennon." He was addressing the man's character, the John Lennon that the public couldn't know, the humanity behind lyrics that were memorized by a generation. A party guest needed cheering up, a morale boost, and Lennon simply felt compelled to make a sad person happy.

"That's what I remember about the Beatles," Ryder said. "Ringo was sort of like a pawn and George may have believed he was a god, but John believed in humanity. You can tell me all the bad things about John Lennon you want, but I don't think you'll find many. Lennon was remarkably consistent in his life, and his career, in his compassion for people."

Ryder cheered up. The party lasted three days, and the Summer of Love had begun. Fall and winter couldn't be too far behind.

CHAPTER SIX

NOW WHAT?

The question on the album cover could be taken many ways: "What Now My Love?"

Released in November 1967 on producer Bob Crewe's newly formed DynoVoice label, *What Now My Love* was the first true solo album by a Wheel-less Mitch Ryder. The title could be taken two ways: What did the audience want from Ryder, and what did Ryder want to be as he grew musically?

It was a confusing time, and Crewe himself seemed uncertain of his own musical direction. He also released during that period an album by a troupe of cheerful singers, the Bob Crewe Generation, with the fashionably hippie-sounding title *Music to Watch Birds By*. It was Crewe's idea, not Ryder's, to include portions of Rod McKuen poetry on *What Now My Love*.

There was a lot to consider with the new album, but it was not a sound likely to find favor with fans of the Detroit Wheels. The group was now effectively—and officially—a memory. There was no specific moment, studio argument or onstage fight that dissolved the original band, no mystery woman who came between friends and partners. One day they were the Wheels; the next day they weren't.

"We went in and cut the first record with all the boys from Detroit," Ryder said. "Two records later, two of the guys were gone. There was hardly any group left, so there wasn't a feeling that something horrible would happen if I didn't record with them."

Bass player Earl Elliott was a U.S. Marine. Guitarist Joe Kubert was unable to work while beginning what would be a lifelong struggle with addictions. Ryder, Jimmy McCarty, and John Badanjek were a band in name only during the group's peak of popularity. McCarty was the only remaining Wheel on "Sock It to Me—Baby," and recordings increasingly were made with just Ryder, separated from the band he had left Detroit with just two years earlier.

McCarty and Badanjek returned to the Motor City and teamed up briefly with other musicians while using the name the Detroit Wheels. In 1969 they released a single, "Linda Sue Dixon," known chiefly for the acronym initials that made deliberate reference—unlike John Lennon's inadvertent "Lucy in the Sky with Diamonds"—to LSD.

The struggle between Ryder, Crewe and the shadow of the band played itself out—literally—on *What Now My Love*. Ryder took the opportunity to add horns for a true rhythm-and-blues, Big Band–influenced sound. There was also room for Crewe's more conventional show business aspirations, with middle of the road ballads drowned in lush arrangements. Short of being a "concept" album, *What Now My Love* offered a choice in musical direction. One side featured Ryder and a respectable cast of blues-based talent, including guitarist Mike Bloomfield and studio veteran Freddy Purdy on drums. Rock and blues-guided songs ranged from a cover of Jerry Lee Lewis's "Whole Lotta Shakin' Going On" to an aptly titled composition, "That's It, I'm Movin' On."

The flip side of the album was pure Crewe. Borrowing a page from the book of producer Phil Spector (chief progenitor of the layered "wall of sound" technique that squeezed half an orchestra into the recording studio), Crewe buried Ryder's voice under complicated versions of standards including, "Baby I Need Your Lovin'," previously recorded by the Four Tops.

"He had all the strings and arrangements and classical shit," Ryder said. "That set the stage: What now? What do you want: rock and roll, or serious performer? The audience had to make a choice, Mitch Ryder had to make a choice, and Bob Crewe had to make a choice about which way we were going to go."

Fans seemed to understand the dilemma, if not its solution. Detroit-area alternative newspaper the *Metro Times* noted years later that Ryder's voice was diminished—not accented—by studio tricks replacing a rock-and-roll band.

"Most people blame Crewe for forcing Ryder to make the love-it-or-hate-it *What Now My Love* a concept album of sorts," the *Times* said, "if that's what you want to call Ryder singing ballads without the Detroit Wheels."

Ryder was frustrated at the final product, particularly given the expanding playground that the other guys were exploring. "In my heart, hanging out with the bona fide artists of the day, I was totally frustrated about not being able to create and write my own material.

Musical choices aside, *What Now* may have felt like just another product in a series. The LP was the sixth Mitch Ryder album, each with ten to twelve songs, in about two years. Even allowing for the brief recording sessions of the era, the output was impressive when added to the nonstop concerts, television appearances and other commitments. The earliest days of fame made for the busiest schedule imaginable.

The career question—What now?—implied more than just which songs Ryder would sing. Inevitably those who can command a stage with nothing but a microphone and an attitude are put to another type of show business challenge: a screen test, to be exact.

Along with his recording obligations, Ryder was under contract to the industry-leading talent pool, the William Morris Agency. Not long after the move to New York, Crewe put Ryder through rudimentary acting classes. When an artist produces a string of hit singles, Hollywood becomes interested. Singing sensations from Bing Crosby and Frank Sinatra to Elvis Presley and the Beatles were among the scores of musicians who made the leap from stage to screen, often with commercial (if not always artistic) success.

Ryder's acting experience had been limited to a high-school theater, not exactly the same thing as auditioning for a role in the MGM cowboy epic *The Wild Bunch*, to costar with William Holden and Ernest Borgnine. "Sam Peckinpah himself came in to direct the test," Ryder said, recalling an arduous process that began before 6:00 a.m. A seat in the makeup chair alone took an hour before Ryder was put through variations of several scenes. A noble effort, but Ryder was not among the finalists for various roles in the ensemble cast.

Ryder was also considered for a smaller-budget film, based on Truman Capote's landmark nonfiction novel *In Cold Blood*. An audition was held to see if Ryder could portray Perry Smith, the pivotal killer in the story. Callback sessions were arranged, and Ryder felt confident of his chances.

"Apparently they were ready to go, but they wanted to take one more look at an actor with a lot of experience," Ryder said. Former child star Robert Blake obviously had more screen time behind him and was given the part. Ryder's crossover into acting would wait for another day. "It was nice to be that close to the finish line," he said.

Ryder took the missed opportunities and close calls in stride. Auditions and screen tests were simply additional conversations in a blur of meetings, phone calls, photo sessions, and interviews. "It was just part of the system," Ryder said. "Most of the young acts that showed up in movies were the pretty guys." Movie screens easily welcomed Fabian, Frankie Avalon or other cute crooners. "I was a rock and roller. Maybe that's why it didn't work. They sang safe songs and broadened that into acting. That was the formula: Make them multi-talented; make them as big as you can make them."

Movie stardom was not a priority item on the Bob Crewe agenda. Crewe's westward vision stopped a little shy of Los Angeles, attracted by Nevada neon. "To my manager, the Holy Grail was Las Vegas," Ryder said. "He just didn't see where the change in music was going."

Crewe was not the only influence hoping to inform Ryder's decisions. Other people had opinions about the singer's career, and some encounters included potential life-changing opportunities. Rock history would have written an interesting, alternative chapter if some of those pairings had come to the spotlight. Ryder became particularly friendly with a rising guitar hero during long nights in the Village, where club-hopping musicians embraced their own inner fan and enjoyed the best seats in the house.

"When Jimi Hendrix was going to dismantle his group, he asked if I would sing with him," Ryder said. "I was blown away by that. Maybe he was just high or drunk, but there was an appreciation of my voice, I guess."

After taking an early discharge from the U.S. Army—Hendrix was injured during paratrooper training at Fort Campbell, Kentucky—Hendrix hit New York in April 1965, just a few months after Billy Lee and the Rivieras began playing Trude Heller's club. Hendrix was working studio and stage sessions for artists including Little Richard, but his own legend quickly grew in the Village bars.

A year later, both singer and guitarist were becoming famous, each in search of a way to push the rock-and-roll envelope wide enough to deliver roots-driven blues. Their similar musical journeys and influences were obvious. By the time their names appeared on the same sales charts, Ryder was among the first to have experienced a sound that nobody else knew an electric guitar was capable of making.

"I got to hear a test copy of *Axis: Bold as Love* before it was given to the record company," Ryder said of the second album by the Jimi Hendrix Experience, released in January 1967. They sat in Hendrix's room, the walls lined with a series of expensive speakers that pushed the boundaries of the new "stereo" presentation. "The mix would carry the guitar all the way around. It was exciting as hell."

Hendrix's reputation was growing, especially among other musicians. In 1967, Hendrix performed in London to an audience that included a stunned Paul McCartney, who heard a unique take on the title song, "Sgt. Pepper's Lonely Hearts Club Band," performed just a few days after the album had been released. A student of blues history, Hendrix was equally comfortable adapting the work of his contemporaries, including the Beatles and Bob Dylan.

"At New York University, I witnessed Hendrix doing, for the first time, his version of 'All Along the Watchtower,' and what a magnificent performance that was," Ryder said. "Dylan was in the front row. I stood to the side of the stage watching his face. Hendrix brought the crowd to its feet, including Dylan."

The careers of Ryder and Hendrix included a common conflict with their associates. The three-man Jimi Hendrix Experience was coming to an end, and Hendrix approached Ryder about a partnership. "He was thinking of breaking up his group, and asked me if I would sing with him," Ryder said. "I didn't take it serious."

The speculative, "what if" game includes considerations besides music: Would Ryder have been able to help, or would he have joined Hendrix in the struggle he was suffering with drugs? "I wasn't into heroin," Ryder said. "I don't know how much of that I could have taken, to be honest. The psychedelic thing (including acid) was experimental, but heroin always carried a dark shadow about it. Don't know where that would have gone."

Another career invitation for Ryder came from *What Now My Love* session player Bloomfield, whose critically acclaimed Blues Project led to the formation of a new group. "Bloomfield came to me when I was on the road and asked me to be part of a group at Columbia, the Electric Flag," Ryder said. "I turned them down, too."

Sometimes, though, getting together with another well-known artist worked. Ryder made many friends with the musicians he met in New York, including an impromptu jam session in a Greenwich Village club with a superstar lineup both onstage and off. The audience consisted of Rolling Stone Brian Jones, Ryder played drums, guitar chords were provided by Stephen Stills and Neil Young, and at center microphone was Otis Redding.

Ryder's musical frustration came from being a fan trying to find a place for his voice. "I was listening to beautiful voices like Otis Redding and Wilson Pickett," Ryder said, "and trying to establish my own sound as well." (There was always room, however, for a tribute version of the songs he admired; the *Break Out . . . !!!* album included a cover of "In the Midnight Hour," written by Pickett and Steve Cropper.)

Ryder crossed paths on occasion with Redding, a Stax Records artist making his pitch to be among the hierarchy of contemporary rhythm and blues. "Everybody knew the king was James Brown," Ryder said. "They were trying to find the prince; it was between Otis, Wilson, and a couple of other guys. There was sort of a battle at the Apollo," he said of the famed Harlem theater.

As 1967 drew to a close, Ryder had the chance to work with Redding. They appeared on *Upbeat,* a pop-music television show based in Cleveland. Redding was fresh from November recording sessions for what would become his best-known song, "(Sittin' on) The Dock of the Bay." Ryder and Redding earlier that year shared chart space, with Ryder's "Sock It to Me, Baby!" vying for singles attention alongside Redding's "Mr. Pitiful." Before the *Upbeat* cameras and a small studio audience, the two performed a duet of Redding's "Knock on Wood," on December 9, 1967.

"The next day, he flew off and died," Ryder said. "I was the last person to perform live with him, if you could call TV 'live.'" Redding perished when his plane went down near Madison, Wisconsin. Within weeks, "Dock of the Bay" became Redding's first and only No. 1 hit single, a timeless classic.

"Otis was truly one of my heroes," Ryder said. "Nobody else ever sounded like him; he had such a distinct style." Ryder enjoyed—on behalf of his late friend—the success of "Dock of the Bay," said to be inspired by "Sgt. Pepper" in the era of psychedelia yet true to its rhythm-and-blues roots. "He was one of the great voices, in the same way that Nat King Cole and Sam Cooke had a distinctive style."

Otis Redding's memory and musical legacy lived on. During a 2006 backstage chat Ryder had with Paul Rodgers (on tour with Brian May and Roger Taylor of Queen) the conversation turned quickly to musical heroes. "You just want to talk about other artists, that's the nature of the business, Ryder said. "We talked about Otis. Of all the things we could speak about in a few precious minutes, it was Otis Redding."

The creative differences between Mitch Ryder and producer Bob Crewe came to a head in 1968. There is no dispute over who asked for the business divorce.

"I finally had enough and said I wanted out," Ryder said. He told Crewe, "You made me a star. I want to be an artist."

Crewe clearly preferred making a star, to include repackaging (yet again) previously unused Wheels recordings by layering a selection of horns on top of the arrangements. The album was released in early 1968, titled *Mitch Ryder Sings the Hits*. (The second Ryder album in a year to have the word 'Hits' in the title.) A new cover picture of a screaming-into-the-microphone Ryder didn't disguise the remakes. Other songs on the album were hardly in step with the post–*Sgt. Pepper* attitude of exploring new territory; Ryder's hard-core fans paid little attention to covers of recent ("Come See about Me") and not-so-recent ("You Are My Sunshine") classics.

Ryder understood that his partnership with Crewe was not likely to insure the longevity of his career. Crewe didn't seem aware of, or interested in, the dramatic changes taking place in music.

"It's one thing to go into a fight without a battle plan," Ryder said of the competition that seemingly changed on a weekly basis. "But if you're going up against a guy who can adapt at will to his environment—and you have a very structured battle plan—the other person is bound to beat you."

Ryder complained more frequently. His objections were brushed aside by Crewe. "His philosophy was, 'I gave you one hit, then two hits, so don't argue,'" Ryder said. "And how can you argue? If it continued to be a success, what were you supposed to say?"

By late 1968, very few in the music industry had not adapted, one way or another, to the changes that were sweeping over everything, including music. Considered a novelty act not too many years earlier, rock and roll was now more than just the featured entertainment on television and in films. Its influence was seen in literature, journalism and other forms of publishing, technology, advertising, and, yes, even politics. Social impact notwithstanding, as a business it was poised to grow larger than even the wildest dreams imagined, and most of the industry recognized that the sock-hop crowd was long gone.

Along the way, the musicians themselves rejected the previous concepts of success, and pushed as hard to make a statement as a dollar. Pop music was no longer separate from the world around it; echoes of Vietnam were heard in song lyrics; if the 1963 assassination of a president stunned American youth into silence, the 1968 murders in April and June of Martin Luther King Jr. and Robert F. Kennedy inspired screams of protest. Rock and roll's teenage audience became young adults, active and engaged in the world around them, demanding that their music keep pace with the times.

Ryder and Crewe clearly looked at the same business from different perspectives. "There were lines now that were becoming harder edged," Ryder said. "Even though I was popular, I was never a 'popular artist.' That's what my producer wanted me to be, and that's what I fought against."

Ryder wanted to be, simply, a great rhythm-and-blues singer. Crewe dreamed of creating another Tom Jones to bask in the Las Vegas spotlights, a tuxedo-wearing idol backed by a big band. Crewe also wanted control of more than just the music and image. He formed the publishing company Saturday Music to provide the songs recorded by artists on his own DynaVoice label—an impresario turned mogul.

"He had a little Tin Pan Alley of his own," Ryder said, referencing the legendary crew of New York songwriters. "He knew his bread and butter were in publishing. Everybody else in the world was encouraging their artists to write, but he didn't want to share a penny of the writing or publishing with anyone."

Though the rift between Ryder and Crewe widened, there were attempts at compromise. In late 1967, Ryder took a new group on the road to Crewe's dream destination, Las Vegas. The performance, however, was not the cabaret crooner of Crewe's vision. Ryder fronted a nine-piece, horn-driven band (who earned a collective total of $250 per week) and played a university arena in Sin City.

"Crewe was excited that I was going to Vegas," Ryder said. "But when I got there and did the show my way, he was very disenchanted. It wasn't a lounge thing like he envisioned; I was doing my rhythm-and-blues show."

Ryder's contract gave Crewe the final word on creative issues, and Ryder wanted his artistic freedom. The friction between producer and singer was put to a legal challenge, albeit a mismatched one. Ryder had scraped together pretty much his net worth—about $110,000—to finance the Big Band tour that followed the Vegas show. Ryder filed suit in New York to recover royalties he believed he was owed. Mitch Ryder and the Detroit Wheels had sold an estimated six million records (albums and singles), yet by summer 1968 Ryder had said he had not received adequate compensation.

In a court of law, the perceived inequity didn't trump a legal agreement. Based on the evidence—being the terms of Ryder's contract—the request for money did not present a solid argument. "We went into court in New York, and he won," Ryder explained years later. "I lost on appeal. Even if I was happy not to work with Crewe, he still owned my contract."

On paper, the Ryder-Crewe lawsuit was a matter of earnings, but the singer said there was more at stake. Dollars could be earned, Ryder figured, but only if his career could continue to flourish. "I was willing to overlook the money if he would just give me my freedom," Ryder said. "That started the split and that horrible fight in the courts of New York."

As in divorce court, where little attention is paid to claims of "He said, she said," the ruling judge felt no obligation to settle artistic differences between a manager and a rock-and-roll star. Ryder's principal objective was of longer-lasting concern: "to convince my producer to allow me to become more competitive with the new rules being introduced into the system."

Regardless of the outcome, there was no future for the Crewe-Ryder pairing. Crewe sold Ryder's contract to Paramount, which offered Ryder options as disparate of the sounds heard on *What Now My Love?*

"They gave me a choice," Ryder said. "You can go to Los Angeles and make a recording with Jeff Barry [producer of the Shangri-Las and the Ronnettes], who was doing sort of pop music. Or you can go to Memphis to work with Booker T and the MGs. Knowing my history, which do you think I took? Given the choice, I want the road with the bumps in it."

It had been a lot of miles between Detroit and New York. Heading south to the heart of American blues, Ryder was ready for a fresh start.

Ryder had a few more odds and ends to take care of. The "big band" that had formed for a series of shows (including the Las Vegas gig) slowly dissolved, one instrument at a time. "The band literally disintegrated, piece by piece, on the road," Ryder said. "When it was down to just a rhythm section, we were in a little club in New Jersey." The musicians took their chances elsewhere, and somewhere off the New Jersey Turnpike, Ryder realized the end of another road.

"I paid the guys their final paychecks, gathered up all the equipment and had a sort of garage sale on the spot," he said. "I remember letting a Hammond B-3 organ go for about $350—maybe 10 percent of what it was worth."

Ryder got his money, left the club, and took a cab to the airport for a flight to England. He spent a few weeks at Lionel Bart's house before returning home, not to Detroit but to Memphis.

In June 1968, under the direction of musician-producer Steve Cropper, Ryder recorded *The Detroit Memphis Experiment,* released in early 1969. Motor City soul meets southern blues, with singles including "Sugar Bee (We Three)," "It's Been a Long Time," and perhaps the album's most memorable track, "Liberty."

The Detroit Memphis Experiment was either ahead of its time or hopelessly out of date. Following the footsteps of *Sgt. Pepper's Lonely Hearts Club Band*, the Beach Boys' *Pet Sounds,* and works by Dylan, artists and groups were abandoning the practice of hurry-up-and-record sessions.

Complex arrangements and harmonies, experimental music, psychedelic sounds, and electronic dreams were captured on vinyl. Those with writing talent set new ambitions, not the least pretentious of which was the term "rock opera" affixed to the Who's 1969 double-LP, *Tommy*. Just making an album of songs didn't seem to be the "in" thing to do.

Some, however, still preferred a pure, bare-bones approach to music. Cropper assembled an all-star group of players including Booker T and the MGs. On a limited budget they made what Ryder called "a rush job. Working at Stax was just another day at the shop."

Among musicians, the Memphis studio was one of music's bright lights, with early stars Booker T and the MGs opening the door to Wilson Picket, Sam and Dave, and "new kids" including Isaac Hayes.

It wasn't, however, the sort of music included in a Dick Clark *American Bandstand* dance party. *The Detroit Memphis Experiment* was aptly named, a formula mixed in a musical laboratory with uncertain results. As an experience, the artist felt rewarded.

"For me it held some magic," Ryder said. "It was something I always wanted to do. Rather than torment myself about my inability to fit in, I chose an arena where I thought I could fit in very nicely. It gave me a lot of insight about how they made those records. Just to play with Booker T and the MGs was reward in itself."

Artistically, Ryder said the results were mixed. It was a working-class, deadline-driven project without a unifying direction. Cropper initiated one way the music could go; Ryder added his opinions.

"Every day we would go up to the little cubicles where the writers were and listen to songs. Then we'd go down and record it," Ryder said. "There was no concept. That's why we called it *The Detroit Memphis 'Experiment,'* because it was thrown together."

Still, the talent came through. Some choice grooves here and there by the MGs, some tightly arranged transitions under Cropper's direction, and a more mature voice from Ryder, far from being the rookie kid in a Manhattan studio.

"There are a couple of brilliant moments," Ryder said. "My favorite is 'Liberty'; everything cooked, everything came together." Technically, he wished there had been more time for the final mix, although that may be a case of the artist hearing the flaws the audience couldn't. "Every time I listen to it I'd find what was wrong with it in my mind."

It wasn't a concept album, but the LP made a statement in other ways. The message to the fans and other musicians was that Ryder was not going to betray his origins, would not become a wind-up Mitch Ryder doll cranking out teenage dance songs.

Admittedly depressed, his contract sold to Paramount, Ryder learned the hard way his place on the pecking order of show business. "The reality that I was a piece of chattel became very real," Ryder said. "I didn't have any control over where I was going to go and where I would be. It dampened my enthusiasm for trying to create something to fit in with whatever was happening."

The album may not have contained "hidden meanings," but statements were made in the liner notes (the text on a record album including credits, appreciations and dedications), in which Ryder referred to the business in less than flattering terms:

"After being raped by the music machine that represents that heaven-on-earth, New York by way of Los Angeles," the message said, "Mitch Ryder is the sole creation of William Levise Jr." Not a friendly note, by any means. Those who were connected with the backstage gossip understood the statement; some may not have cared for the opinion.

"That was a mistake. I would pay for that," Ryder said. "Those very powerful people do not like to be ridiculed or tampered with publicly. It's something you don't do if you want to keep a career."

By the time *The Detroit Memphis Experiment* was released in early 1969, Mitch Ryder was, as claimed, the property of William Levise Jr. Now he just had to determine who Mitch Ryder was and if he still wanted to carry the name.

CHAPTER SEVEN

"FREE OF SOCIAL RESTRAINTS"

The Sixties were coming to an end: a screaming, crashing train wreck of a halt. Not everyone survived the dying decade; the funeral procession that had started in 1969 took a few years to complete.

A generation's achievement was on display when it viewed its own planet from a considerable distance. America's glory of walking on the moon offered an ironic contrast to a troubled world. One minute there was national pride in watching Neil Armstrong's July stroll on the moon; the next report offered sorrow and shame through a daily death tally of fallen soldiers in Vietnam.

It had been a long road for the nation—politically, socially, and culturally. When the decade began, Mitch Ryder tested the waters of singing publicly, with the modest ambition of entertaining, making crowds dance (regardless of race), and seeking a common beat people could understand. The music business changed dramatically in the years since; so had everything else.

Ryder during an Ann Arbor concert, 1970, with the band Detroit. (Photo courtesy of Mitch Ryder.)

Rather than return to New York after the release of *The Detroit Memphis Experiment,* Ryder went back to Detroit. The professional marriage to Bob Crewe—and Ryder's identity as front man for the Detroit Wheels—was over, the only reminder being a single released on the AvCo Embassy label, reissuing "Jenny Take a Ride" backed with "I Never Had It Better." The song was given a second wind when it was featured in the movie *C. C. and Company,* starring Ann-Margret and football player Joe Namath in the title role of C. C. Ryder (complete with honorary spelling).

The Wheels were no more though; 1967 was a memory and so were the musicians Ryder once worked with. The Wheels were just another group to dissolve in Ryder's life: The big band fell apart one brass piece at a time, and *The Detroit-Memphis Experiment* was a one-time-only gathering of players and talent. Ryder was without a band, management, or direction.

Avoiding the show business enclaves of New York and Los Angeles, Ryder teamed up with a colleague who also hailed from the (hopefully) welcoming Motor City. "There was a comfort there," Ryder said of going home. "The people knew what we had done: We carried the name of the city in good faith, gave a positive light to it, brought a lot of joy to people, and sold a lot of records. Whatever transgressions I might have been guilty of, people in Detroit were willing to forgive while New York wasn't."

An avid music enthusiast of varied interests, Barry Kramer's talents included a budding career in publishing. Ryder and Kramer had briefly met during a 1966 photo session. Kramer the photographer took pictures of swimwear-clad pop stars for a teen magazine, a pictorial spread that featured the young leader of the Detroit Wheels.

Rejecting New York's position as the Great and Powerful Oz of the Printed Word, Kramer was determined to operate in Detroit, and his vision for a rock-culture magazine would recognize the city's contributions to music: not the blues or Motown but the grinding guitars and screaming vocals, arguably best summed up by Mitch Ryder. New talent made local names for themselves in the wake of the Wheels' success: rising revolutionaries the MC5, guitar-wielding assassin Ted Nugent, and a determined singer-songwriter named Bob Seger.

Kramer was also savvy enough to recognize a market when he saw one; the record bins were filled with more mature, driven, and inspired music than during the teenybopper days of yore. It was time to also expand the reading consciousness of its listeners, and *Creem* magazine was launched out of Detroit, hoping to mirror the success of other publications. Publisher Jann Wenner survived that crucial first year since the November 1967 launch of *Rolling Stone,* giving space to everything from John Lennon's thoughts on Vietnam to renegade writer Hunter S. Thompson's dissertations on paranoia. Kramer's accomplices for the publication included future stars of music writing, including Lester Bangs and Dave Marsh. *Creem* would carry an attitude that other publications avoided, Kramer thought, and as a business could include the production of music and promotion of artists.

Fresh from the *Detroit Memphis* sessions, Kramer saw the album's single "Sugar Bee" capture respectable reviews, but he also learned that a rhythm-and-blues album may not have been the best product for the changing market. He struggled to promote sales, and thought Ryder's talents could be put to better—or at least more lucrative—use.

"He wanted to create a rock-and-roll group to get me away from rhythm and blues," Ryder said. "He came up with the idea that would eventually become Detroit." What better title for a band to carry the city name into a new decade?

Whatever was going to happen, though, needed to begin soon. Ryder was without an income save for what he earned on the road. Before taking an act on tour, Ryder needed musicians, a strategy, and a direction. Kramer was involved with a variety of players in the still-viable Detroit music scene, as *Creem* magazine emulated *Rolling Stone* in covering both the musical and political worlds. With diverse contacts (notorious, in some cases) Kramer stepped in to guide the next phase of Ryder's career.

"The first thing he saw was that my finances had been cut off but my liabilities and responsibilities were ongoing," Ryder said. The two worked their way through reams of paperwork to take financial pressure off Ryder, buying time to form a proper plan.

The first idea was the obvious one: put the Wheels back on the road.

Since they last performed together, things had changed. Bass player Earl Elliott was no longer interested in the life of a professional musician. In 1970, guitarist Jim McCarty began a two-year run with the group Cactus, which had been formed by former members of the defunct Vanilla Fudge. Rhythm guitarist Joe Kubert, who first explored music with Ryder in junior high school, was also contacted without success.

"Joe was interested but had his problems," Ryder said. The drug use that began as a way to avoid the draft rendered Kubert unable to perform. "He didn't last very long. It was clear there were going to be some problems."

Drummer John Badanjek was available, but without the others it was decided not to call the group the Detroit Wheels. Since the phrase "Mitch Ryder and . . ." wasn't going to be used, Ryder hoped that *this* time the group would loom larger than the singer. "I didn't want this to be about Mitch Ryder," he told Kramer. "I just wanted to call it 'Detroit' and decrease my profile and visibility."

The name on the LP was a decision that could wait. First they needed a sound and an album. Musicians came and went, and by 1970 a semi-stable group had become a band. Guitarist Steve Hunter signed on, a versatile player who would later record with Lou Reed and Alice Cooper. Harry Phillips and W. R. ("Ron") Cooke provided keyboard and bass. Others floated in and out of the lineup on hazy dreams of music stardom. By the time they were ready to tour, a beaten-looking group of players and hangers-on had been made into a seven-man band.

In many ways, it was starting over for Ryder, but it felt like the same old thing. Ryder remained under contract to Paramount, which expected some product from the hit-maker they considered their property. The Hollywood studio was trying to loom larger in the music world, Ryder learned, with limited success.

"Paramount was not a real powerful record company," he said. "As a record studio, they made wonderful films." The sound and image that came, literally, from Detroit may not have been what Paramount expected from a dancing, singing pop star carved in the *American Bandstand* image, the kind immortalized in four inches' worth of plastic and silver lamé

The group Detroit (*left to right*): Steve Hunter, John Badanjek, Mitch Ryder, Ron Cooke, and Brett Tuggle. (Photo by Leni Sinclair.)

jumpsuit. Then again, the Beatles were no longer the head-bobbing Mop Tops of 1964; they began the new decade by breaking up.

The times had a-changed by 1970. Music was about far more than simply getting a date with Peggy Sue; recreational drugs sometimes became deadly addictions; and the war that in many ways marked the decade came home to America.

Long before a band tries to capture its sound in the recording studio, it helps to know what that sound is. Billy Lee and the Rivieras played hundreds of shows before being recorded in Manhattan, and however experienced some of the players now assembled, the group had to start from the beginning.

In early 1970, Detroit began playing small gigs, from a high-school dinner in Terra Haute, Indiana, to whatever clubs in Detroit survived the '60s. The glory days of the Village and other venues were mostly a memory—the 1967 riots in downtown Detroit further defined the rift between city and suburbs, which relocated the music clubs to farther reaches north and west of the city. Tensions eased somewhat during the Detroit Tigers' 1968 World Series victory, but after the celebration white fans went home to the suburbs while African American city residents were left in a crumbling metropolis that had once been among the brightest in the nation.

Whether or not the band was ready for national attention, the singer's name earned them a place on marquees and concert posters. That spring, Ryder and the unlikely group hit the road for a tour of the South under the name Detroit, a band of outlaws as hard as the guitar riffs heard on the song "Rock and Roll."

"The band lived up to their image," Ryder said. "It was a rough street band. Two of the members were bikers; there was a lot of drugs, a lot of hard living."

The band's habits weren't much of a secret. The new worlds of journalism and celebrity allowed for admission to all things, acknowledgment of any behavior. *Rolling Stone* and *Creem* didn't bother hiding the drug use of interview subjects (or the writers themselves). Rick McGrath's music column in the alternative press, the *Georgia Straight*, featured a July 1970 review—of sorts—of a concert in Vancouver. A road-weary Ryder told McGrath a story about the band's stay at the Holiday Inn. The after-show party turned into a drugged, drunken orgy in rooms adjoining those of family vacationers.

"It was just ridiculous," Ryder recalled with a scowl. "Worse than you can imagine. Here's some people going down the hall with their little kid, and some fucking long-haired motherfucker was walking around with his prick hanging out. Walks by and says, 'Hi,' like nothing was going on. Ten minutes later, some chick's running down the end of the hall, yelling she's being raped by two guys."

Life on the road: screams from hotel rooms, marijuana smoke filling the halls, amplified instruments heard round-the-clock, naked women a common sight. "One of the guys shit into a bag and threw it out into the street," Ryder snapped, neither making a joke nor disguising personal disgust. "Every sacrilegious move that can be made was made."

By comparison, the paper airplane pranks of Billy Lee and the Rivieras killing time in a New York hotel room were more than just innocent; they were a harmless reminder of simpler pleasures and easier laughs. In half a decade, the worst elements of rock and roll (and all that it reflected) graduated from spirited rebellion to open defiance.

In some cases, the escalation was also dangerous. The concept of music concerts in this new era of "rock" (older listeners in their twenties abandoned the childish-sounding "rock and roll" in favor of more serious sounds) achieved the rare distinction of actually creating something new: the pop-rock festival. Why stage a ninety-minute show for a few hundred teenagers when hundreds of thousands were just as willing to buy tickets for a two- or three-day bacchanal? Power to the people.

The days-long festival of songs, open drug use, social awareness, guilt-free sex, and a generation in search of itself (or all of the above) was born with the Monterey Pop Festival to celebrate the Summer of Love, 1967. Organized by producer Lou Adler and John Phillips of the Mamas and the Papas, the three-day event in southern California welcomed more than 200,000 fans eager to expand their consciousness. The acts delivered: the Who and Jimi Hendrix respectively smashed and burned guitars, and the lineup included Janis Joplin, Otis Redding, Simon and Garfunkel, and Ravi Shankar, the Indian sitar player who taught the instrument to George Harrison.

Two years later, an estimated half million stoned souls camped out at the upstate New York farm of Max Yasgur, near a town called Woodstock. The good news, even among those who snubbed their nose at the sight, sound (and smell) of Woodstock's legions, was that a small city's worth of hippies could commune in a contained space for three days without disaster.

The bad news, in December 1969, proved that theory wrong. The Rolling Stones hosted a free concert at the Altamont Speedway near San Francisco. The Stones employed members of the Hell's Angels motorcycle club as bodyguards—a decision that doesn't require hindsight to be considered foolish—who consumed their payment of an obscene amount of beer before the show. It wasn't a successful mix of sensibilities, and the "security" included the beating death by the Angels of a fan. (Stones singer Mick Jagger is captured viewing the tragedy in the documentary *Gimme Shelter*, his stunned reaction an accurate, helpless portrait of the end of the decade.)

Much of Michigan's Midwest sensibilities were less than embracing of a pop festival. By the time Mitch Ryder's Detroit was announced as the top act for a three-day rock orgy in Goose Lake, a small town in southern Michigan, there was reason to be concerned about these gatherings of young people. War protests—ostensibly the "theme" of Woodstock—did more than just bring the anti-Vietnam movement to the public's attention. On May 4, 1970, the war itself took place at Ohio's Kent State University. Four students were shot and killed in what National Guardsmen believed was becoming a violent protest organized by the radical Students for a Democratic Society. The SDS was not on campus that day, but four unarmed civilians—students—fell victim to American bullets.

The "generation gap" was treated as if it were a war. When faced with the moral dilemmas that divided the country, some Americans assumed—of course—that rock music was the root of all modern evil: Goose Lake was not a welcome idea.

"I am a concerned citizen interested in the welfare of our younger generation, and highly alarmed about the effects of the recent wave of so-called pop concerts," a Grosse Pointe resident wrote in an Aug. 1, 1970, letter to the *Detroit Free Press*. The end of the world, he predicted, would begin Aug. 7 at Goose Lake. It wasn't going to be pretty. "This will provide an opportunity to be free of social restraints for three days," he explained,

Power to the people: Ryder onstage in Ann Arbor. (Photo by Robert Matheu.)

"and will set the stage for orgiastic revelries, including the use of dope. No thinking person can question the adverse effect this has on the moral fiber of young people."

In spite of the Altamont tragedy, concert-festivals flourished. "Happenings" covered the map from peaceful Middlefield, Connecticut, to Chicago's Grant Park, home to a "riotous" festival headlined by Sly and the Family Stone. Those who couldn't attend a weekend-long blowout that summer turned movie theaters into smoke-filled stand-ins when the film *Woodstock* hit screens. That it played to sold-out (if hazy) audiences helped, from a business standpoint, keep festivals flourishing.

For Goose Lake, promoters expected 100,000 people. Twice that number showed up, having purchased $20 tickets at Detroit's venerable Hudson's department store in response to newspaper advertisements headlined, "Dear Brothers and Sisters."

Little was written in the southern Michigan or metro Detroit newspapers about the artists or the music in the days leading up to the event. Instead, letters predicting Armageddon shared space with reports of Michigan Attorney General Frank Kelly's attempts to stop the concert, a legal maneuver that failed in court. Kelley made a public-safety argument that was countered by Goose Lake property owner Dick Songer's commitment to having seventy paid security guards on hand. (Editorial space was a precious commodity that week: President Richard M. Nixon risked having a mistrial declared when he pronounced defendant Charles Manson "guilty"; elsewhere in the nation's courts, a grand jury was convened to study the tragedy at Kent State.)

Behind-the-scenes negotiations to make Goose Lake a reality were many, said promoter Russ Gibb, a veteran radio disc jockey and club owner. Gibb's long tenure at pop station WKNR/ "Keener" joined cultural history when he was credited with launching the rumor that Beatle Paul McCartney was dead and that clues could be found by stoned album owners combing the lyrics and images for confirmation. Gibb matched his radio fame with ownership of Detroit's Grande Ballroom, and booked shows with local legends and international stars alike, whether introducing Ypsilanti's Iggy Pop or playing host to the premiere performance at the Grande of something called a "rock opera," when the Who debuted *Tommy*.

From the audience, a festival may have appeared to be just a matter of the groovy people getting together with their friends, some of whom happened to be recording artists (but just like them, or vice-versa). Behind the peace signs (both painted and hand-shaped) and amplifiers, Gibb served as a buffer between the hip and the straights, meaning those who controlled things like permits, licenses and the law.

"We knew what was gonna happen when these kids would come in," Gibb said. "We had transportation, road studies, surveyors, health control . . . We tried to cover all bases." Medical teams were on hand, Gibb said, a heightened need given the refreshments served and consumed at such outings. Treatment for such emergencies posed its own unique problem, for which Gibb and the police agreed upon a strategy.

Gibb met with officers from the Michigan State Police in Lansing (a

Ryder onstage at the People's Ballroom in Ann Arbor during a period of management by John Sinclair. (Photo by Robert Matheu.)

meeting attended by a representative of the governor), and while all agreed that the kids liked the music and no one was out to "get" anyone—love between young people and police officers was more than usually strained in light of recent events—they couldn't just let felony crimes go by without at least trying to arrest someone.

It wouldn't be easy. The odds of a few cops, even a handful, trying to drag a suspect away from a supportive crowd (which included more than a few dozen drunken thugs, criminals, and borderline psychopaths) didn't seem to favor the officers. Instead, it was suggested, the discreet, undercover (sometimes crew cut–wearing) officers in the sea of hair would report the obvious drug dealers to state troopers, who stood cross-armed outside the gates, batons and handcuffs at the ready.

"They decided it would cause a riot if they started making arrests in the park," Gibb explained. "They said, 'We'll have our guys in there to spot certain people.' We thought we could handle it ourselves; our guys were cooler because they were probably dopers themselves. They wouldn't be too aggressive." A compromise was reached, the logistics and legality of which were debated briefly in the days following the concert, but by then the show—and the scene—had come and gone without incident.

Billed as Michigan's Woodstock, Goose Lake's lineup included Jethro Tull, Joe Cocker, Chicago, Ten Years After, the James Gang, and Brownsville Station. For hometown pride, Gibb sought the biggest Motor City name he could get. "His name was well known," Gibb said of putting Mitch Ryder near the top of the concert posters. "We wouldn't have put him on if he wasn't."

Gibb was inclined to think big for the festival, which was taking place on nearly three hundred acres of property being developed, an amphitheater built, and a lake dredged. Of this challenging and expensive project, said Gibb: "We bought a $40,000 dollar plow, and it fell in the goddamn lake. We were never able to get it out."

A counter-culture city was born, however short-lived its destiny. Gibb understood that those strange young people might look alike but subdivisions existed within the Aquarian unity. Separate parks were built: a motorcycle lot, "The Toke-A-Lot," hippie heavens, and musical paradises each having their own sections of grass to smoke grass upon.

"It was like building a city," Gibb said. "It took us months and months to get that together. *Billboard* said it was the best festival they ever attended: It went off on time, due to Tom Wright and his stage crew." Gibb praised the circular platform that allowed the equipment of the exiting group to be spun behind the curtains for adjustment while a fresh setup of drums and amplifiers was brought to the center of the stage. From a security standpoint, keeping some form of distraction/attraction onstage as much as possible reduced the risk of too much idle time for the 200,000-plus waiting for a show.

Just how much time on stage a band would get was a different matter and not a script that was carved in stoned. The musicians reflected the audience's nonchalance regarding a structured schedule.

"I pretty much went out to party," said Ryder, who allowed himself an acid trip for the event. He played with Detroit, and with Teagarden and Van Winkle, session men who were then recording with rising star Bob Seger. "I found myself waking up in their trailer. They asked if I wanted to play with them, and I did. I did that with several musicians. There was no time limit; that was the beauty of music then; the audience had no expectation about how long you could, or should, play."

Formats and philosophies were changing for concerts as they were in publishing, movies, recordings, and, naturally, radio. Upstart radical FM stations ignored the AM conventions of song length and category designations, and musicians made records that demanded equal time onstage before a live audience.

"They had gotten into long, extended album plays on FM," Ryder said. "You could hear songs that lasted ten, twelve, fourteen minutes. It wasn't unusual to carry that to your performance."

On paper, the talents involved with Detroit were the right group at the right time to take advantage of an eclectic market, an appropriate description coming out of a festival that featured the gravelly voiced blues of Cocker and flute-based instrumentals from Jethro Tull. What was being written and said about the artists—in the era of *Rolling Stone,* FM radio,

Onstage at Goose Lake,
August 1970. Along with
the Detroit band, Ryder
shared the stage with
other musicians during
the festival. (Photo by
Leni Sinclair.)

and feature films that mined rock for soundtrack music—was as important as what was heard on record.

With Barry Kramer, Ryder thought he had found the answer to the
Bob Crewe career-management question. "Kramer's connections in publishing gave us a credibility," Ryder said. "He did a public relations trans-
formation that was quite successful, turning Mitch Ryder and the Detroit
Wheels into the group Detroit. It was like reinventing Mitch Ryder."

After Goose Lake, it was time for the band to record. Sessions were held in both Detroit and Toronto for a selection of songs far rougher than even the inspired howl on "Devil with a Blue Dress On." Included were a remake of the Rolling Stones' anthem, "Gimme Shelter," and a blistering treatment of Lou Reed's "Rock and Roll."

The recorded product might have stood the test of time, but the group and its personalities weren't meant to go the distance. Behavior on the road, on tour, had always been suspect, often rowdy, and sometimes criminal. With Detroit, it was the same story in the studio, amplified to near feedback levels. The Toronto recording sessions for "Long Neck Goose" were beyond Ryder's worst nightmares. The work dragged on for days longer than necessary, schedules were ignored, and recreation took center stage when the hangers-on took the place of musicians.

The front lobby of the studio building featured full-length glass walls that faced the city sidewalks. Returning from an errand, Ryder saw what the music world offered the public when a crew member took center stage facing the street. "He was in total view of all the passers-by," Ryder said. "He had a big bottle of champagne sitting by the side of his chair. Nestled between his legs was his girlfriend, giving him a blow job. The people walking down the street couldn't believe what they were seeing. That freaked us out."

Reportedly, while the amateur peep show was offered to the citizens of Toronto, Ryder later heard that a fourteen-year-old female guest was having a private moment with a band member. "Turns out one of our musicians was screwing her upstairs," Ryder said.

The behavior escalated and multiplied as sessions dragged on. Back in Detroit, Kramer was less than amused, as was Ryder. "He thought he was running into some creative, energetic musicians, which he was," Ryder said. "But he was also running into some totally uncivilized, immoral descendants of Vikings or something."

Recreational drug use throughout rock (and society) became ugly, sometimes deadly. Within weeks of each other, on September 8 and October 4, 1970, Ryder's friend Jimi Hendrix and rising blues singer Janis Joplin died from drug-related incidents. Some took it as a wake-up call; others escaped further into drug-fueled denial, and a few more would follow in the same tragic footsteps. (The Doors' lead singer, Jim Morrison, died the following year, joining Hendrix and Joplin in death by age thirty.)

For Ryder, "the show must go on" was a business obligation as much as a trouper's dedication, the necessary evil overshadowing the inspired art. The singles, "Long Neck Goose" and "Rock and Roll," earned favorable reviews, and Kramer made good on his plan to provide media attention to the work.

"The press party in New York at the Rainbow Room was outrageous," Ryder said. "He was able to make us a media darling. It was a high-profile deal and got everybody's attention."

Detroit's handling of "Rock and Roll" was called by songwriter Lou Reed "the way it was supposed to sound." The album was heard widely in Canada, a contractual understanding since much of the recording took place there. Ryder seemed, again, ready for liftoff into famous atmospheres. "In all the hip places, like San Francisco, we got a lot of play," Ryder said. "It was sort of a grass-roots thing, but it never really blossomed into a full commercial bloom."

The success or failure of Detroit—the group and album—lay on Ryder's shoulders, justifiably or otherwise. The singer lobbied in vain for the group credit on the LP's cover to read simply *Detroit*, arguing that three of the songs were performed by other vocalists from the band. Paramount insisted, however, and won the battle when *Detroit . . . with Mitch Ryder* was released.

In the 1960s, there were those who sought to use Mitch Ryder to make money. Heading into a new decade, others tried to use his musical popularity for other purposes.

One of the first specific "causes" adopted by pop musicians—shortly before some bravely turned rock's attentions to true humanitarian efforts—was questionable in its intent, if not its nobility.

The arrest, conviction and sentencing of John Sinclair became a cause to champion by the hip and musical. In 1964, Sinclair—a poet, writer, and musician—formed the Detroit Artists Workshop based out of Wayne State University. Sinclair had recently been arrested for possession of marijuana, and his opposition to the country's stringent pot laws (and, arguably, consumption of same) fueled a passion for other political causes.

After a second arrest for marijuana possession in 1966, Sinclair served six months at the Detroit House of Corrections. The following year, Sinclair was busted yet a third time in what the Wayne State newspaper called, "Hippie dope raid on campus."

Sinclair was also a would-be poet and reporter who wrote for the counterculture underground publication *The Fifth Estate*. He established a more aggressive periodical, *Guerilla*, a magazine for social upheaval. Publishing aside, Sinclair helped launch the White Panther Party, a revolutionary civil-rights group sympathetic to the by-any-means-necessary Black Panthers. Along the way, his involvement in the local music scene included booking gigs for the MC5 and arranging concerts at the Grande Ballroom.

In July 1969, Sinclair was again sentenced for pot possession, a seemingly disproportionate ten years for possession of two joints—marijuana cigarettes—that became a rallying cry among young activists (who avoided mention of Sinclair's three previous convictions for drug possession or sales). Sinclair was released in 1971 when the state overturned his conviction after Sinclair's folk-hero status was certified in a John Lennon ballad; concerts were staged to help free the writer, including Grande Ballroom gigs and an Ann Arbor appearance by Lennon and Yoko Ono.

Fresh from prison, Sinclair returned to the activist group now known as the Rainbow Peoples Party, a mixed bag of social protesters, artists, and—under its own management team—musicians. Sinclair attempted to parlay his underground name recognition into music management, beginning with the group Detroit. Through Barry Kramer and those affiliated with Detroit-area publishing, Ryder was a passing acquaintance of Sinclair's and would now become business partners, of a sort.

"Barry was under a lot of pressure to dump the band, and we had another album due," Ryder said. "Then comes John Sinclair." It made as much sense for an activist to manage a band as anyone else in those hazy days of the decade change.

"In the 1970s—or the late '60s, as I call the early '70s—music was essential to how we communicated with each other," said Harvey Ovshinsky, a writer and publisher who founded *The Fifth Estate*, which included Sinclair's name on its masthead. A veteran observer and participant in the Motor City musical, political, and cultural scene, Ovshinsky said that outlets for the youth movement, from concerts to radio stations to the printed word, shared what they considered a common goal.

"There was a sense of community with publishing, politics, and music all blended in with the movement," Ovshinsky said. "We were all going to be arrested by the same police; we might as well be together."

That togetherness attracted Sinclair, who had visions of using music to express (and fund) his revolution. Along with managing the MC5, Sinclair thought Ryder and Detroit could help further the cause, perhaps with more mainstream appeal. Sinclair was eager to link up with what he saw as the proper mix of music and attitude. Bass player Ron Cooke told an interviewer about the energy Detroit brought to the party, including a few performances at "Free John Now" concerts, with lineups featuring the MC5, Bob Seger, and Ted Nugent's Amboy Dukes crowd.

"The real Detroit band was the live, no-holds-barred party band," Cooke said. "We did a Christmas gig in Boston that was unreal. They had to call the police on the place to shut it down; it was going right through the roof, man. It was a good gig."

Ryder believed working with Sinclair made some sense, although the name recognition of Sinclair did not necessarily translate into quality contacts in the entertainment industry. "That was a mistake," Ryder said. "He had no esteem in the music business; he had notoriety and a lot of credibility in the underground press."

It made an interesting combination. Sinclair the writer was famous for being famous—recognized more for pot than poetry; Ryder was linked (forever) to being the guy who sang "Devil with a Blue Dress On." Promoting the group was made easy by recognition, even if the work wasn't always given proper exposure. "We were being seen everywhere, quoted everywhere, but nobody heard our music," Ryder said. "Sinclair was a bit opportunistic about that."

Ambition and political-social philosophies merged into something of a commune, housed in what Ryder called Sinclair's "mansion" in Ann Arbor. Ryder was pulled into a world he may have sympathized with but found no comfort in. If Ryder thought former producer Bob Crewe's lavish lifestyle and outrageous excess were a waste of money, the hypocritical mentality of Sinclair promoted a comparable disgust.

"They paid all that money to rent that mansion, then went out and did fun things like dig huge craters in the front lawn to represent the bombs that had fallen in Vietnam," Ryder said. "They were very theatrical."

Barely surviving in a Royal Oak apartment, Ryder was invited to live in the carriage house behind the mansion. In spite of the communal spirit, Ryder recognized a capitalistic side to Sinclair and Company. "They wanted three or four times the rent we were paying for our apartment," Ryder said. "That was the beginning of not being enamored with the communist way of living. I didn't like having to go to them for money I was earning. I was a good hippie; I just wasn't a good communist. I was too Americanized."

Sinclair had more success with the hard-edged group the MC5—a band with an underground reputation that struggled for mainstream success, given that their most well-known song began with the declaration, "Kick out the jams, motherfuckers." Even the upstart, rebellious FM stations couldn't clear that one for airplay.

"It wasn't like I was the MC5 and bought into John's dream and then found success," Ryder said. "I already knew what the trappings of success were."

Ryder also knew the downside of fame, being its sudden absence. He was still in his mid-twenties—young by most standards but much older after five years in the music business. His lifestyle had been downgraded, he said, from just a few years earlier when he had been on the "A" list of Manhattan's social life. "It was a bitter pill to swallow," Ryder said.

Artistically torn between his beloved rhythm and blues and providing commercial success, financially on shaky ground with contracts claiming different ownerships of his work, and personally drained from five years on the rock-and-roll road, Ryder and Detroit disintegrated for reasons that had nothing to do with music. Ryder was expected to turn over concert fees to the collective Sinclair crew, but bookings as Mitch Ryder and Detroit were becoming scarce without a direct pipeline to concert promoters. In theory, Ryder understood the intention of using music to encourage the youth revolution, but reality demanded that bills get paid, contracts met, and obligations fulfilled.

"At the time, the alternative press was the political extension of the hippie movement, and the arguments being put forth by the leftist, liberal-leaning hippie community were valid arguments," Ryder said. "But they were dreams; dreams for a dream world. They weren't based anywhere in reality."

Some of those dreams were nightmares. The group Detroit included in its cast and crew a post-office wall's worth of borderline criminals, the band's finances and recording contracts were subject to industry blackmail, and at least one individual was sought by the Federal Bureau of Investigation: a frequent face at the mansion commune was Lawrence "Pun" Plamondon, cofounder of Sinclair's White Panther Party. In 1968, Plamondon made the FBI's Most Wanted List for conspiring to bomb the Ann Arbor office of the CIA. Ryder heard the news of Plamondon's 1970 arrest on the radio.

"I thought: Maybe this isn't such a good group to hang out with," Ryder said.

The music industry wasn't as enamored with Detroit as it had been when the Motown stars cranked out hit after hit; the band carrying the town's name seemed to mirror a beaten, struggling city. For its March 2, 1972, edition, *Rolling Stone* magazine sent writer Ed Ward to spend time with the group, both during a performance in Indianapolis and at home, where the band's raw energy impressed the reporter more than the town itself.

"The city's got a soaring crime rate, an outrageous heroin market, some of the most vocal political fringe groups in the country, and lots and lots of cars," Ward wrote. During the reporter's visit, he naturally checked out the rolling circus that was Woodward Avenue, filled with those homegrown vehicles, "hell-bent for nowhere in particular."

Ward followed the group's caravan to the Hoosier state, where an outdoor venue, a racetrack, awaited Detroit. About fifty riot-prepared police patrolled the audience ("lots and lots" of cops, as Ward might have said), joined by hovering helicopters and horse-mounted officers waiting for an excuse to let loose. Detroit's show came the day after what *Rolling Stone* called "another rock and roll riot" during a free afternoon concert by Canadian group the Guess Who, a solid, rocking band on the rise but not known for inciting violence or negative energy.

Maybe that was all the energy that was possible; no posturing or party attitude could change the fact that an era had ended. No amount of rallying by young people prevented the reelection of a president who would barely shake off his second inaugural hangover before whispers were heard about misdoings in the Watergate hotel. The ashes of burned draft cards hadn't prevented the military deaths in Vietnam to surpass fifty thousand before the United States did the (to many Americans) unthinkable: walk away from a war the loser. The party was over: Rock and roll was here to stay, in one form or another, but the toll it took on its stars kept a separate tally of victims.

No money, no control over personal finances, no progress with recording or performing music—Ryder wasn't the only musician that year in search of a new band, a final handhold before accepting the inevitable decline of a decade.

The MC5 was at the end of their reign as the rebellious bad boys of Michigan garage rock. Formed in 1964, the "Five" pounded out their defiant shows and rowdy records until the final months of 1972, when the band dissolved one member at a time. Founding member and guitarist Wayne Kramer started the New Year as if a long-term relationship had just ended, all dressed up with nowhere to go. "I moved in with a couple of musician friends," Kramer remembered, accepting the hospitality of bass player Tim Shafe and guitarist Mark Manko at their Hamtramck home. Shafe and Manko were veterans of the band Detroit and made the guitar player feel welcome. "I was fundamentally homeless, musician-style," Kramer said. "The band breaks up, and if you don't have a girlfriend to crash with, so you move in with your buddies. They let me stay in the basement."

Shafe, Manko, drummer K. C. Black, and other musicians were informally playing with Ryder at sessions held in the Hamtramck home, inspiring a natural invitation for the basement guest to, "pick up a guitar." "It seemed like a natural fit," Kramer said. "I was 'at liberty,' so I joined the band."

The Knock-Down, Drag-Out Party Band lived up to their descriptive name in smaller towns and hotels through the final months of 1972. Kramer soon realized that his ambitions for the group weren't likely to happen with an informal cast that combined legitimate musicians with, in a rotating group, semiprofessionals at best. The members shared habits more than harmonies.

"'Knock-Down, Drag-Out' was not an inaccurate description of the lifestyles of the musicians," Kramer said. "It was pretty loose. But I've always been fairly ambitious, always had a grand scheme in mind. I saw that some of the players were the wrong people for the job, but the core was pretty good."

Neither Kramer nor Ryder could be considered rookies, and starting over as a bar band seemed pointless, given their credentials. The veterans disagreed over the lineup and, in some ways, purpose of the group. Kramer said Ryder called it "not righteous" to think that better musicians should replace friends in an attempt to earn a decent living.

"That's what happens when you have neighborhood friends and old buddies," said Kramer. "The line was blurred between people who can really play who are committed to doing the work, and people who are there by the luck of the draw."

Kramer presented his argument to Ryder, and accepted the rejection. "I couldn't argue with him," Kramer said. "He was the lead singer; it was his cache that was carrying the day."

The band dissolved and reformed through a half-year's worth of occasional gigs, but the ingredients weren't in place for a successful operation. The inevitable results of the addictive lifestyles ended any speculation of what the band might have become.

"Anytime substance abuse is practiced with that enthusiasm, it's almost impossible to do any real work," Kramer said. "Knock-Down was a problem because it really was a hard-drinking, hard-drugging outfit. It's real work that makes bands achieve anything, not how much dope you do or how many glasses of whiskey you drink on the night of a gig. We didn't know anyone that didn't take drugs, that today we would call 'clean and sober.' Everybody got as high as humanly possible all the time."

There were no hard feelings when this band—one in a series for many of the players—took its final bow. That's not to say Kramer walked away without some regret.

"We never really got to develop the music," Kramer said. "We started to try and write a couple of songs together, and I was very excited about that. He's such a great singer; I had a lot of belief in him. I knew what I could bring to the table in terms of songwriting and guitar playing and how to make a good record, and what he could bring with his incredible voice and great good looks and charisma. This could be something really exciting; but, like I said, we were too high."

Prospects for the band were too few, too late in the game. Ryder couldn't bring himself to believe that the music industry would give him another chance, even if he were to make the effort. Those he called "enemies" in the business ran too deep for him to invest himself into a new beginning. His heart just wasn't up to another fight.

Ryder struggled with a decision to turn his final bow into an extended intermission. "I walked away from it," Ryder said. "I said: That's it, I'm done, there's got to be a different way. I lived through it, but it wasn't pretty."

Still obligated by contract to Paramount for a follow-up to the Detroit album, Ryder mulled over his options during a visit to New York. Following a meeting at a Central Park concert by the J. Geils Band, Ryder entered into a brief, ominous business partnership with Bud Prager, manager of the hard-core trio Mountain. Few contracts begin with a prediction of such a personal, harsh nature:

"He told me I would end up hating him," Ryder said.

There may have been other factors at work, Ryder believed. The upside

Ryder belts out a song as the first period of his public life neared a hiatus that began not long after this 1972 show. (Photo by Leni Sinclair.)

was that Prager made good on his promise to get Ryder released from his Paramount obligation, removing the pressure to put together an album. The downside was that Ryder was left without management or a label to call his own.

Admittedly "on my last legs," Ryder wondered what else could happen to a career that seemed as mismanaged as it was poised for greater stardom. Prager booked a few engagements; Ryder dutifully performed, fading recitations with a rotating band at gigs including the Wild West Shows headlined by Leslie West and Mountain.

There are more than two sides to the stories that followed. A conspiracy designed to force him out of the business, Ryder maintains, cast him with the reputation of being difficult to work with and limited the exposure to a voice and sound that seemed to have proven its worth. Ryder was unable, again, to connect with the right manager at the right time. Dating back to the day Bob Crewe obtained parental signatures on a contract that turned William Levise Jr. into Mitch Ryder, the singer felt betrayed by those he trusted. Managers, promoters, booking agents, and other contacts became what Ryder saw as enemies; the stress had taken its toll.

"I was being brutalized," Ryder said. "Leaving music for whatever reason is serious. I felt compelled to leave." As the decade came to a screaming, crashing halt, the singer who would forever be connected to the 1960s soundtrack was a tired young man, old at age 28.

"I didn't want to quit music," he said. "I just didn't want to be Mitch Ryder anymore."

SECOND ACTS

CHAPTER EIGHT

FLIP SIDE

"You're Mitch Ryder. What are you doing here?"

That was a frequent question put to William Levise Jr. during a five-year hiatus from the public stage. People were surprised to find Ryder—and he was, in fact, Mitch Ryder—working in a Colorado warehouse during the mid-1970s.

What was he doing there? A valid question. The repetitive strain of forklifts and pallets, of loading and unloading trucks was not, Ryder's co-workers thought, what they would do if they had his voice, name, or talent. Loading-dock dreams are tempered by reality with each shipment to be hauled off or wrestled onto a truck; the never-ending task of Sisyphus understood by factory workers mindlessly repeating each day's efforts.

Why was Mitch Ryder spending his days as an hourly warehouse employee? Taking a long overdue break, among other things, a reassessment of his ambitions. Ryder's retreat from the business of music allowed for the apprenticeship of a craft and art that he hadn't completed. The potential of his voice was noticed at an early age, but fame required its payment in product long before the artist was allowed a proper education. During the years a vocalist should be given a chance to explore musical boundaries, Ryder was carved into a pop mold that forever cast his likeness as the singer of two-song medleys and rhythm-heavy hits.

For five years, Ryder spent his requisite hours at the warehouse, went home to a family dinner, and stayed up late in a private world of his own creation. He wrote, taking a stab at a semiautobiographical novel as well as poetry and lyrics; painted (including respectable canvases that would eventually be seen on album covers); introduced himself more intimately to the guitar; and learned to play the clarinet.

"I couldn't wait to punch out," Ryder said, a statement heard at countless factory time clocks bolted onto cinderblock walls. "I would come home and work myself to exhaustion on creative efforts, out of frustration and desire; there was a lot of hurt that I dealt with by creating."

It was never meant to be a permanent separation from the show that had been his life, just an intermission while the star took another look at the script. "It was clear, from the day I left music, that it would never last," Ryder said. "It was all about preparing to come back."

There were opportunities to return earlier from his self-imposed exile. Ryder was approached to sing with Rare Earth, ironically the first white group signed by Motown Records, which in 1972 relocated to Los Angeles. The band scored several hits with covers of Motown classics, including the Four Tops' "Get Ready" and their own feel-good anthem, "I Just Want to Celebrate."

Ryder flew out to Motown's California offices for an audition at the request of Rare Earth's manager, Cholly Atkins—a former Motown choreographer. Come out to the coast, Atkins said. No obligations. Maybe see Disneyland, hang out with the guys, play some music.

It wasn't that Ryder had no interest in returning to music, but the mid-1970s music scene in Los Angeles was one of open drug use practiced by those in management as much as by the musicians themselves. It scared him; the environment was perhaps a more polished version of the rampant drug use that surrounded the Detroit band, but the fast-lane

Alone in the spotlight, Ryder's feelings for the industry never affected his enjoyment of the performance. (Photo by Leni Sinclair.)

life included the same temptations that were part of his decision to step offstage.

It was the business—not the music—that Ryder avoided. Musically, he couldn't stay away too long. In Colorado, he formed a part-time band, playing small concerts before audiences ranging from prisoners to a group of mentally challenged adults.

"This one poor soul fell in love with me," Ryder said of a woman at an adult care facility. "She wouldn't let go of me when it was time to leave. They were literally dragging me out of the building with her gripping me." The business may have caused countless disappointments, but connecting to the audience still provided the singer with pleasure.

"It wasn't that I quit music," Ryder said. "I couldn't stand the idea of not performing. I had never forsaken music. If anything, it was ripped away from me."

After five years, Ryder decided to take back his rightful place in professional music, to grab what had been ripped from him. Musically, he felt confident in his determination; from a business standpoint, the Sixties were decidedly a long-ago, hazy memory. The rebels no longer had a cause (they thought); the fashions and tastes of American youth abandoned the dope-smoking, long-hair, blue-jean–wearing crowd in favor of the cocaine-sniffing, platform-shoed disco set. Movies of social rebellion were replaced with slicker traditions: *Star Wars* was inspired more by old-time Hollywood than any counterculture agenda; *Saturday Night Fever* warped the marriage of music and movies away from issue-oriented rock to mass-market appeal.

The market, and the business, changed, but so had the singer. Ryder was no longer a wide-eyed twenty-year-old dwarfed by New York skyscrapers and blinded by penthouse views of Fifth Avenue. He came back but was determined to do it on his own terms.

"I felt like I was underwater trying to hold my breath all those years in Colorado," Ryder said. "I jumped into the air and took the biggest gasp of life I ever felt. I made the decision to breathe again, that's how important music was to me. I was suffocating by staying out of music."

The first order of business was to form a company, a label of his own creation, even if the name sounded like a Sixties anachronism: Seeds and Stems Records. Perhaps there was a dual meaning: seeds to represent new growth; stems a solid branch of support.

On the other hand, consumers of marijuana recognize the disposable parts in a bag of pot; the portions cleaned out before the leaves are smoked. "It was shameless pandering to the drug segment of the population," Ryder admitted.

The concept, however, was valid, allowing for complete control over his art. Ryder would have final authority over the music, but he knew that "solo" referred only to the act of singing onstage. He needed help and began a partnership with two men, keyboard player Billy Csernits and Tom Conner, a budding producer with a passion for the hometown music scene.

A veteran musician from the early 1960s folk community in Detroit, Conner had worked briefly with Mark Frost and Grand Funk Railroad, a band based in Flint, Michigan. Conner produced an ambitious compilation album, *Michigan Rocks,* including cuts from Frost, Bob Seger, Ted Nugent, and the MC5. Ryder's first new song in half a decade, "Long Hard Road," appeared in the collection, inspiring Conner to seek more material from Ryder.

"He approached me about doing an album of my own here in Detroit, with local backing," Ryder said. The career decisions, however, would be Ryder's and Ryder's alone. Seeds and Stems would provide the label, the music would come from Ryder, and a band he nicknamed the Thrashing Brothers, featuring Csernits, drummer Wilson Owens, bass player Mark Gougeson, and guitarist Wayne Gabriel, a veteran of the Elephant's Memory band that backed up John Lennon in the early 1970s.

"Billy [Csernits] convinced me that, no matter what happened, I owed it to my public, the people who loved my music, to reenter," Ryder said. "I had already determined that, but he reaffirmed it for me."

Csernits urged the musician in Ryder, while Conner, the more experienced of Ryder's new colleagues, provided a safety net of trust. Ryder and the band put songs together for an album. This time, he was determined, he would maintain control over the work.

"It was a bit of an ego trip, but it was the only way to protect myself," said Ryder, no longer filled with insecurity and prepared to take on all responsibilities. He would decide what the cover looked like (the first being a Ryder painting of a hippie-looking person contemplating a portable radio with a Rocky Mountain background); how the liner notes read; the balance of songs that gave room for both autobiographical statements and allegiance to rhythm and blues. "I insisted on having control of every facet. I was going to be the master of my own destiny in all those areas where I had been disappointed and fucked over."

While Ryder's comeback album was being prepared, it was time to take the most public step in his return: appear onstage. Performance dates in Canada allowed Ryder to reacquaint himself with the music world. Small bars in southern Ontario towns—London, Kingston, wherever; Ryder played entry-level gigs while working up to larger halls in Vancouver and

Saskatchewan. The reviews were warm, welcoming as always to the powerful voice onstage.

With his new band, the shows offered a combination platter of old and new: Obviously "Jenny" and "Devil" were requisite songs, enjoyed both by the singer and the audience; the climate in 1977, however, allowed for, even encouraged, new music, including "Long Hard Road" and other songs from the album-in-development.

At first, Ryder balked at playing before American audiences. Conner convinced him that the American fans would welcome him, using the positive notices from Canadian shows as his trump card. "I had been refusing to play in America because of the way I suffered in the industry," Ryder said. "Tom said, 'Look, the people love you.' He got me a gig and said if I didn't like it we wouldn't have to go back."

On June 29, 1978, the announcer at San Francisco's Old Waldorf Theater introduced the singer: not a band, no mention of Wheels, just "Ladies and gentlemen, from Detroit, Michigan, Mitch Ryder."

Stepping into that spotlight was, Ryder said, "the biggest monkey off my back I'd ever experienced." Reviews raved that Ryder brought the house down, a confirmation of his ability to continue becoming an artist and not, "living in the shadow of a manufactured star," he said.

Most gratifying of all was the response—and the songs that inspired the reaction. "The people went nuts," Ryder said, "not for 'Jenny' or 'Devil' but for the new album. That was the first date in America, which led to other things."

Naturally, a Detroit-area gig was in order, and Ryder was booked for three nights at an Ann Arbor club, the ironically named Second Chance. Hometown applause never sounded as sweet. Ryder's onstage confidence (always present regardless of the circumstance) disguised his remaining doubts. He wondered if the audience's screaming, shouting support was, in part, a note of sympathy for the abuse Ryder claims he suffered from the music industry. Given the casual interest paid by most music fans to business-oriented, non-gossip news, it seems more likely the enthusiastic response was simply for seeing a hometown hero who had survived.

"I deluded myself into thinking they knew what the industry did to me and were showing their support for me," Ryder said. "In reality, maybe they just hadn't seen me for so long. Maybe it was a mixture of both."

Freelance writer Crispin McCormick Cioe wrote about Ryder's return for *Detroit* magazine, and watched all three performances. The reporter joined audiences that included former Wheels Jim McCarty and John Badanjek and members of Bob Seger's Silver Bullet Band. "More than 500 people dressed more for a disco than a rock show," Cioe wrote, a sad observation how much had changed since Ryder last took the stage.

The burning question remained: Was there room in the late 1970s for veteran rockers, whose "oldie" records were played on AM radio while air time on "contemporary" FM stations was dominated by the newcomers? Ryder opened the show with "Jenny Take a Ride," but concentrated on giving his new material a public test.

The fans were fickle, bowing to fashion one moment while demanding rock and roll in its purest form the next. Detroit audiences, Cioe observed, wanted both: "raw emotion along with smoke bombs and dry ice." For those who listened, Ryder was as good as ever, if that was still the measurement of a performance. "One of the strongest, most emotional voices on the radio, period," Cioe said of the show.

In 1979, the Seeds and Stems label released the album *How I Spent My Vacation,* nine pieces of musical autobiography cowritten by Ryder (teaming up lyrically with his wife, Kimberley, and musically with guitarist Gabriel). Singles included "Nice 'n Easy" (featuring guest drummer John Badanjek of the original Detroit Wheels) and "Freezin' in Hell." It was more than just a respectable return. *Rolling Stone* magazine called the album a "masterpiece," joining a chorus of enthusiastic reviews and "welcome back" messages.

The musicians on the album were encouraged about the prospects for a revived Ryder career, including guitarist Gabriel, who hoped that the work would generate commercial interest to go with the critical appreciation. Gabriel was a rookie ("a baby at the time," he said) when he briefly joined the first version of the Detroit band: the years since found Gabriel on stages and in recording studios backing the likes of John Lennon and Mick Jagger.

Gabriel said Ryder's insistence for artistic autonomy (and turning his business dealings over to Conner) and personality conflicts may have prevented the late-1970s incarnation from reaching its potential. "Mitch has had so many opportunities to do one thing or another, and he's tried to always go his own route," Gabriel said. "I don't think we recorded the album we should have; we were always at odds with each other offstage, but onstage we were pretty tight."

As the 1970s drew to a close, the music business held little tolerance for those seeking simply to make music, and the lack of business acumen worked against Ryder's comeback.

"Like most of the artists from that era, Mitch was his own worst enemy," Gabriel said. "But I loved working with him. We wrote well together, and the energy onstage was just unbelievable." Gabriel speculated that Ryder was cautious about plunging too deep into business matters that previously had been tended by Bob Crewe or other managers. "At the time, I thought he put it in other people's hands who did not make the right decisions for him. I was very frustrated most of the time. We should have been more on a national level than we were. He could have rose to that occasion." (Ironically, when Gabriel parted company with Ryder, he was approached about joining a band called Limousine to be managed by Bob Crewe, an arrangement that was never realized.)

The fans, however, weren't as eager, and Ryder said that financial success—however welcome it would have been—wasn't the goal. "The beauty of *Vacation* was that it was an artistic accomplishment, but it wasn't commercial," Ryder said. "Any good reviews were applauding me as an artist, trying to give me some encouragement to go on."

Torn between his past and a potential future, Ryder's return to show business opened the doors to old and possible new friends. After the release of *Vacation*, Seymour Stein, a veteran promoter with an eye on what was being called "new wave" music, contacted Ryder for possible management and representation. Stein headed Sire Records, a label with a notable roster including Chrissie Hynde and the Pretenders and David Byrne's Talking Heads. Stein was able to recognize and develop talent, most evident in

Ryder performs "Rock and Roll" with writer Lou Reed at the Masonic Auditorium in 1978. Reed called Ryder's treatment "The way it was supposed to be played." (Photo by Robert Matheu.)

turning four unrelated guys of limited abilities into the Ramones, a watered-down version of the era's so-called punk bands.

Stein was on a roll, especially when he signed a young woman whose popularity began in lower Manhattan's dance clubs, a Michigan-born singer who would need only one of her four birth names to be recognized: Madonna Louise Veronica Ciccone.

In the post-Beatles era, Madonna's ascension to fame may have been the closest thing to the "mania" sought by so many and accurately reflected the changing values of artists and their audience. During her debut on *American Bandstand,* Madonna said her ambition was "to rule the world," and she declared with neither shame nor modesty her self-assessment as a "Material Girl." Not exactly an "All You Need Is Love" kind of message for American youths to adopt.

Ryder turned down Stein's offer, the latest in a series of "what if" considerations dating back to near-miss screen tests and a proposed partnership with Jimi Hendrix. Ryder was wary of New York managers and preferred to take the artistic success of *Vacation* to the next level while maintaining control of his business affairs. The business was slick, as always, but lacked the outlaw quality that gave rock and roll its meaning. "It wasn't the rebel anymore," Ryder said. "It was the rebel co-opted."

So-called corporate rock had taken over. In 1977 the record industry generated $3.5 billion in revenue, a 28 percent increase from the previous year (which, in turn, surpassed its predecessor with double-digit increases). Nearly 700 million units (albums, cassettes, or singles) were sold that year—just in the United States. There was more than just gold records in them thar hills.

Fortune in popular entertainment included looking back as much as a search for the "new wave" of music. Nostalgia for the 1950s and early 1960s was in vogue, a trip down memory lane that included the movies *American Graffiti* and *Grease,* the latter of which featured a doo-wop soundtrack that helped revive the career of Bob Crewe's star, Frankie Valli, who sang the title song. In movie theaters, *Animal House* was the unexpected hit of the year (and easily the most profitable given its skeletal budget), further encouraging people to celebrate a youth that may not have been their own.

Logic suggested a reunion of Mitch Ryder and the Detroit Wheels. A complete return of the original band was not possible. Since dissolving in 1967, the Wheels traveled different roads. Guitarist Joe Kubert and bass player Earl Elliott were no longer in the business. After the band Detroit dissolved in 1972, drummer John Badanjek took up with the Rockets under the coleadership of Wheels guitarist Jim McCarty. The Rockets scored modestly as a regional band and flirted on occasion with the national spotlight with hits including "Oh Well" and "Turn Up the Radio." A total of six Rockets albums were released, one on RCA, another on Capitol, and four under the direction of Robert Stigwood's growing enterprise. Still, the group couldn't crack the national charts on a regular basis and individually sought other pastures. By 1978, Badanjek and McCarty were available for a reunion of the band that made them famous.

The reformed Wheels sold out Pine Knob, an outdoor venue about thirty miles north of Detroit. Half the audience was seated in orderly fashion under a pavilion roof, the rest preferring a sprawling summer night on a sloping hill perfect for listening to music (among many other things).

The match-up was destined to be a three-way struggle. McCarty and Badanjek insisted that Ryder do vocals on Rockets tunes. ("I hated it, but it was part of the compromise," Ryder said.) Ryder was anxious to put his new material to a public test; the audience obviously was ready to dance and scream to twelve-year-old hit songs.

"It wasn't meant to be," Ryder said. "It was fun, being with two of the original members. It's always great music. But, I felt that it was going backward to become part of a group after all I had done to remain a solo artist."

Nostalgia was just part of a growing entertainment business that by its nature sought greener, newer pastures. One of the strongest new voices of the era was officially dubbed "the future of rock and roll" when his face appeared simultaneously on the covers of both *Time* and *Newsweek* magazines the same week in 1975. Bruce Springsteen, a gravelly voiced New Jersey–born singer and songwriter, was a much-needed answer to the glitzy tendency of pop stardom for boys so pretty they might as well have been girls (the so-called glam era). As Ryder had been a contrast to the Monkees-style, Beatles wannabes of the Sixties, Springsteen and the powerful E Street Band provided straight-ahead rock with tough poetry that showed sentiment while screaming a defiance of convention, a combination best heard on Springsteen's 1975 album and single, "Born to Run." Whether or not rock's entire future rested on his working-class shoulders, Springsteen offered a uniquely American style born as much of Pete Seeger as Elvis Presley.

Unlike the artists of the previous decade, Springsteen wasn't in a rush to push a new album to the market following *Born to Run*. He resisted giving in during a contract dispute after his first major success and did not release a follow-up until 1978's *Darkness on the Edge of Town,* a three-year delay that would have written the obituary of even the most popular 1960s artist.

Careers, however, were no longer shaped in the Bob Crewe mold of "beating the pony until it can't ride anymore," as Ryder summarized his output of six albums in two years. Rock and roll was here to stay, and artists planned to stick around for the long run.

Springsteen epitomized the changes that the 1970s witnessed in concert appearances, with grinding, sweaty, three-hour marathons that were unheard of in the days of pop shows and multi-act festivals. Springsteen's show was particularly interesting to Detroit fans when he sold out Cobo Hall. His part-concert/part-revival meeting concluded with what he called "The Detroit Medley," taking the Wheels' formula even further by slamming together portions of "Jenny Take a Ride," "C. C. Rider," "Good Golly, Miss Molly," and "Devil with a Blue Dress On" into a frenzied fresco of rock and roll celebration. Springsteen and other rockers of the era gladly acknowledged influences that weren't the obvious choice (meaning Elvis Presley or the Beatles), ranging from Ryder to Roy Orbison.

Ryder was invited to share the Cobo stage with Springsteen during what seemed a nonstop touring schedule. The future of rock and roll was

Onstage with "The Boss": Ryder jamming with Bruce Springsteen during a 1981 show at Cobo Hall. In tribute, Springsteen included "The Detroit Medley" in his late-1970s concerts. (Photo by Robert Alford.)

courteous to Ryder's influence during afternoon rehearsals in a nearly empty arena.

"We went in a day early to do the sound checks," Ryder said. "Springsteen came into the dressing room to just shoot the shit, but he had to do some press and stuff. He treated it very professionally. He made sure I was taken care of. He was very considerate of me; he's just a real considerate guy."

Ryder admired the career decisions Springsteen made and dismissed any accusations at the time (absolutely proven false since) that "The Boss" was a "manufactured" star. "There was a feel about him," Ryder said.

"When you looked at the lyrics, the energy and the quality of the talent, he was the real deal."

The 1970s ended with Ryder as a legend without a manager, famous but unable to find the formula that would again put him with the elite (temporary or otherwise) names jockeying for radio time or chart positions. The marketing and promotion of an album and a talent was now a slick, determined formula, the artists and their art sometimes living in a bubble of denial separate from the world around it. A generation of young Americans had no war to concern themselves with, no focused enemy that represented "the Man" in as complete a way as Nixon had, and no unifying cause specific to their age group. The nation adjusted its priorities during the transitional presidency of Jimmy Carter and spent much of 1979 counting days along with a special news program, *Nightline*, dedicated to the hostage crisis in a previously little-known country, Iran. The politics most favored by rock and roll—typically Democratic in vote, liberal in cause—failed to hold national dominance. The 1980 election shifted American sensibilities away from the "us" decade of the '60s or the "Me" generation of the '70s into a return to conservative posturing.

Perhaps, Ryder thought, the place to go with his new music was not in America. Treated as an "oldies" singer in his native land, Ryder began developing a relationship with fans in Europe, specifically, Germany.

Multiple-act festivals may have had their day in America—the "arena rock" showcases of the late 1970s preferred a main star and opening act rather than upward of a half dozen bands or singers crowding the bill— but the festival was alive and well in Deutschland. Concert marathons were as much a part of German culture as the weeklong beer orgy Oktoberfest.

The Rockpalast concerts beginning in 1979 quickly became legendary for the intensity and lineups (artists ranging from Dire Straits to Rory Gallagher to Dave Edmunds filled the bill), both for the music and the excess that was its companion. Ryder, in charge of a young band experiencing international travel for the first time, was among the highlights of the first series of Rockpalast blasts.

"For them, it was a chance to see the world," Ryder said, himself no longer wide-eyed at new places to see, visit, and conquer. It was, however, somewhat daunting when he was told that the expected audience for the televised Rockpalast shows throughout Europe would reach upward of 170 million people. Keyboardist Csernits was in his early twenties, a foreign man in a foreign land, treated like a star.

"Talk about culture shock," Csernits recalled in a Rockpalast interview. The band had been flown in a week before the gig and were given a chance to see some of the country before taking one of its stages. "A very nice thought, but for a fast, hard-hitting rock band, it was way too much idle time. Great food, carte blanche for everything from room service to massage girls—we were a little on the edge to say the least."

The extent of partying rivaled that which had dominated life on the road in the 1960s; but Csernits never forgot the musical moments. "When Mitch was 'on,' there was always a spot where the music took on a life of its own. The nights when the real Mitch Ryder came to the party were some high points in my life."

Ryder's appearances represented both the highs and lows of life on the road. Musically, critic Alan Bangs dubbed Ryder's show, "a nice surprise," with a nod toward the *Vacation* album that framed the set list. "Listening to the album, you can tell how fruitful the *Vacation* must have been. [Ryder is] one of the few white singers that understands rhythm and blues; he is 150 percent energy." In contrast to the more fashionable, strobe-light theatrics that were becoming the norm in America, the critic called Ryder's show "sweaty, bare-chested, hard-rock, bump-and-grind sexuality."

On the other hand, some called it "Mitch Ryder's ugly hour." The concert harkened back to the behavior and appetites of Goose Lake, with a backstage fight threatening the scheduled start of the show, a "non-interview" Ryder gave Alan Bangs, and an audience that wasn't too receptive when Ryder first gripped the microphone. "Surprisingly, though, it came to be an incredible show," the review concluded, citing, "The intensity all of this brought to his songs." Bangs, unable to solicit a straight answer

The scream remained the same: Ryder belting one out during a 1980 Cobo Hall performance. (Photo by Robert Alford.)

from Ryder before the performance, still called it, "One of the best shows I have ever witnessed."

For Ryder, the applause was sweeter still because of the appreciation for his new music. Bangs said he felt goose bumps while listening to a live performance of "Ain't Nobody White," a song planned for the *Vacation* follow-up album, *Naked But Not Dead*. (The lyrics were taken from a comment once made by Ray Charles: "Ain't nobody white can sing the blues, except the Jews." Ryder heard that "new wave" singer Elvis Costello made a derogatory comment about Charles and his opinion. Bonnie Bramlett, of the duo Delaney and Bonnie, heard Costello's remark and reportedly punched him in the face for insulting Brother Ray.)

It was the best of both worlds overseas: Rockpalast crowds enjoyed the performances of Wheels hits or a cover of the Doors' "Soul Kitchen," but they equally cheered new material and a show that included Ryder jumping to the beer-soaked floor of the audience, putting an arm around a fan for an impromptu duet.

Is it possible for a rhythm-and-blues performance to be too strong, too impassioned? Bangs asked the question: "Some claimed Ryder went too far, that he put more into this than was fair to the audience." Bangs tried his hand at psychoanalysis, observing that the performance revealed "the tension that existed during the whole show between Mitch and his band, but also the [tension] between William Levise and his alter ego, Mitch Ryder."

Bangs missed the point. As the Seventies gave way to a new decade, Ryder and Levise were no longer just inseparable; they were one in the same.

The success in Germany opened the door for Hamburg-based Line Records to distribute the Seeds and Stems product, including *Vacation* and *Naked But Not Dead*. The albums may have had a limited marketing and promotion budget, but for the first time in his musical life Ryder had the freedom to explore his talent.

"What I loved about Germany was they allowed me to become an artist," Ryder said. "They expected me to bring in my own material, to write music. In my earlier career, I was never allowed to do that."

Released in 1980, *Naked But Not Dead*—again featuring a Ryder-painted canvas on its cover—earned respectful reviews but little revenue; the absence of a hit single made the product more popular among musicians than fans. Ryder's determination to chart an artistic career that matched his previous commercial success was appreciated back home by a singer whose name previously appeared at the bottom of late-1960s concert posters dominated by the Ryder name.

If a music industry award were given for sheer perseverance, an appropriate recipient would be Bob Seger. Beginning in the 1960s, the Ann Arbor–born singer was a local favorite, a regular at every venue that survived the city's transition from the '60s to the '70s. Few fans outside of Michigan knew the Seger name, until a run of mid-1970s albums— *Beautiful Loser, Live Bullet,* and *Night Moves*—rewarded him with national success. *Live Bullet* stayed on the album charts an astonishing three years and is considered a classic among concert recordings, and the single "Night Moves" was the first in an impressive series of Top Ten hits.

The man who scored a hit with the song "Rock and Roll Never Forgets" was true to his own lyric. In 1980, Seger sold out Detroit's Cobo Hall for six nights in a row and, against his management's wishes, included an opening act that paid tribute to Detroit rock and roll.

"Bob heard my second comeback album," Ryder said, "and insisted I open for him. That started a little war. The manager and record company pushed for another band. Bob hung tough, and I opened all six nights. That said something to me about Bob: No matter what any of us from Detroit might have to say about each other, we have that sort of regional, hometown camaraderie. Like: He may be a fool, but he's our fool."

Motor City fans are notoriously stubborn, rowdy, and protective of their own. It's a tough city, not always pretty or polite. In the days leading up to the Seger-Ryder concerts, Detroit Tigers President and General Manager Jim Campbell temporarily closed the 10,500-capacity bleacher section at Tiger Stadium (the "cheap seats") owing to an increasing rowdiness among fans. The *Detroit Free Press* published a photo of a visiting team's outfielder surrounded by cups, paper, and other garbage thrown by disgruntled fans that turned the bench-seat sections into a corner bar. (Campbell's disgust—and the shifting sensibilities of American media— were evident when he told the *Free Press* he was "just goddamn fed up" with the fans, a comment printed verbatim in a family newspaper.) It's a Detroit attitude, in an era where local fairs included charity fund-raisers that allowed people, for a dollar a whack, to take a baseball bat to a Japanese automobile. The Motor City answer to an economic problem was not just to work harder and make better products but to trash the competition as well, symbolically or otherwise. The growing threat of imported automobiles to the local economy was just another version of the disrespect Detroiters felt from the nation, and the world, and they clung to their own. ("If you can't beat 'em, beat 'em up" may be the unofficial Motor City motto.)

A concert bill of Ryder and Seger was Detroit's version of Rock and Roll Heaven, played over six nights beginning June 14, 1980. It was, as Seger described in a phrase immortalized by an underwear-dancing Tom Cruise in the movie *Risky Business,* "old time rock and roll."

Outside of the Motor City, however, old-time rock and roll was no longer the path to success. There were few challenging lyrics of social statement to be found among a top Ten that included *Urban Cowboy*–inspired line-dancing rhythms. While Seger seemed to have perfected the formula for hit records, Ryder entered the 1980s as head of a small label struggling to get product into record stores. Ryder and Conner made separate deals with distributors in different regions of the country, but the return on investment wasn't keeping pace with the inflated expense of nurturing a record company into profitability.

"We put out a jazz album, a country album, and two Mitch Ryder albums," said Ryder, the artist referring to himself as just another product line. "We couldn't resolve the cash flow in terms of getting our hands on the money to continue to grow."

In 1981 Ryder released a package of studio songs, *Got Change for a Million?* (published by American Jade) and the concert-recorded triple album, *Live Talkies,* which avoided Wheels hits in favor of an eclectic collection, including a cover of Bob Dylan's "Subterranean Homesick Blues." In

Photo session for the *Smart Ass* album cover. The top right photo was selected. (Photos courtesy of Mitch Ryder.)

1983, another studio compilation was issued, *Smart Ass,* the third album of songs written or cowritten by Ryder. Conner and Ryder restructured Seeds and Stems into a publishing company, Michigan Broadcasting Corporation, determined to have control over every single aspect of his career.

Recording sessions were long, tiresome affairs. Ryder was in the studio with weary musicians after a twelve-hour marathon of recording when he tried to talk to his partner, Conner, in the control room.

"Everybody was tired," Ryder said. "The band was tired. I was barely getting anything out of them. Tom was up in the control room; he had his cowboy boots propped up on the console."

Ryder addressed his partner through the microphone. "Tom," Ryder said. "Tom, we need to talk."

No answer. Ryder replaced the microphone and climbed the steps to the control room to confer with his partner. "He had his boots up on the console, but he was sleeping on the couch," Ryder said.

Perhaps the thrill was gone; maybe it was time for a change.

CHAPTER NINE

OLD "DOG," NEW TRICKS

Many aspects of the 1983 music business were different than when Mitch Ryder became famous; some things hadn't changed at all since William Levise Jr. changed his name and became a "star."

The formula starts with basic talent—a voice matched with the sheer nerve required to stand before a crowd armed only with a microphone and an attitude. Bring in the handlers, experts, managers, and promoters; adorn the talent in stylish clothes, arrange the hair just so, and (if need be) attach a stage name to catch the public's interest. Thus a soulful singer is transformed into the musical answer to young girls' dreams or the reflection of teenage boys' misunderstood angst.

As it was in the mid-1960s, so it was a decade later for Indiana-born singer and songwriter John Mellencamp, clearly a difficult name to fit on an album cover. Under the dangerous (yet cute) sounding "Johnny Cougar," Mellencamp debuted with the 1976 *Chestnut Street Incident,* featuring covers of classic rock tunes "Oh, Pretty Woman" and "Jailhouse Rock."

Neither that album nor its follow-up, *The Kid Inside,* generated much interest, but Mellencamp hit the charts with the 1978 single "I Need a Lover." Subsequent albums failed to produce a song to match the early success, and Mellencamp began doing battle with his record company over the teen-dream marketing of his image.

Mellencamp's industry clout changed in 1982, with the album *American Fool,* and a pair of Top Ten hits: "Hurts So Good" held the No. 2 position for six weeks (running against the No.1, *Rocky III* theme by Survivor, "Eye of the Tiger"); the album's second release, a Springsteen-worthy saga of young love, Midwest style, "Jack and Diane" reached No.1 in October 1982, briefly giving Mellencamp two of the top Top Ten chart positions.

Mellencamp pushed for more than just the ability to use his birth name on his recordings (which would finally be included on the 1984 album, *Uh-Huh*); he was among a new breed of intellectual-but-tough rockers delving into producing, with an ear toward making records with their rock-and-roll influences. Bruce Springsteen oversaw a project for Gary "U.S." Bonds, and Tom Petty supervised an album featuring Del Shannon, the singer from Grand Rapids, Michigan, whose early 1960s hits included "Runaway."

When Mellencamp visited Detroit radio station WABX during a promotional tour for *American Fool,* hometown hero Mitch Ryder was present and accounted for on a poster decorating the station wall. Disc jockey Jerry Lubin, a former road manager of Ryder's, was interviewing Mellencamp when the young singer remarked on his admiration for Ryder. (Mellencamp once opened for Ryder at the Center Stage in Canton, Ohio, but that was before becoming one of the anointed hit-makers in America.)

"John said how I was a great influence and all that stuff, and that he wanted to make a recording with me," Ryder said. "He didn't know Lubin knew me. He was kind of trapped into doing the album."

A meeting was arranged, giving Mellencamp the chance to hear Ryder's recent work. Ryder recognized the power Mellencamp wielded in the industry on the heels of a successful record. "Mellencamp was on top of the fucking heap in America," Ryder said. "His album went platinum, all kinds of stuff."

Mellencamp brought Ryder down for a visit to Indiana. They talked music, naturally, but also talked about about a business where they shared a common experience. Mellencamp was in musical limbo with regard to a follow-up album for *American Fool,* owing to contract disputes with his record label. Temporarily unable to record his own work, Mellencamp was looking to expand his horizons. Actors want to direct; musicians want to produce.

"He could go on tour, but he couldn't record," Ryder said. "One clause did allow him to produce other artists, so he took advantage of that. He told me he was picking between me, Eric Burdon, and Donovan."

Material was selected from some of Ryder's compositions, including "Code Dancing" from the *Smart Ass* album. In early 1983, work began on *Never Kick a Sleeping Dog* at the Shack, Mellencamp's emerging studio in Seymour, Indiana, a farmhouse in the process of being converted into a recording facility.

The musicians were mostly of Mellencamp's choosing, including his own studio players along with guest appearances by other artists. Gina Shock, drummer for the all-girl group the Go-Go's, sat in for several sessions. For the song "A Thrill's a Thrill," Ryder was vocally paired with Marianne Faithful, known more for her relationship with Rolling Stones front man Mick Jagger than her own career, which began in 1964 with a recording of the Jagger-Richards composition "As Tears Go By." Faithful struggled to build her own reputation as an artist, and her 1979 album, *Broken English,* earned critical admiration but generated little commercial success.

Ryder was of mixed opinions about his work with Faithful, for which the sessions took a break from the Indiana winter in exchange for Miami sunshine. He was impressed with her voice if not her professionalism. Told by Mellencamp to "baby-sit" the singer, Ryder (and Mellencamp) patiently worked with Faithful, whose struggles with drugs—including heroin—were an issue and would be until Faithful found sobriety in 1987. Some critics applauded the duet, a harsh, bitter testament to living on the edge. Written by Bill Amesbury, the lyrics to "A Thrill's a Thrill" were particularly poignant when sung by survivors of rock-and-roll excess: "I will try anything, if it makes my head go round."

Ironically, neither Ryder nor Faithful had ever reached the heights of success, specifically in terms of financial reward, that Mellencamp enjoyed. The business offered far greater potential to Mellencamp and his contemporaries than was available for Ryder in the 1960s. Mellencamp himself was amazed at the monetary rewards, receiving during their time together his first royalty check for *American Fool,* which Ryder said was in the hundreds of thousands of dollars. "He was so excited," Ryder said of Mellencamp sharing the news. "I don't think he was doing it to gloat; he was astounded that so much money could be made."

The sessions for *Never Kick a Sleeping Dog* were sometimes difficult, as the best ones are, a clash of cooks believing theirs to be the better recipe. Ryder told the *Detroit Free Press* that Mellencamp initially tried to guide the voice as much as oversee the technical production.

"He had to get in tune with my perspective," Ryder said. "If we hadn't gotten complete control, it could've been a John Cougar record. Finally he backed off. He was able to overcome his artistic personality. When I saw that boy work in the studio, I knew he was a producer."

Keeping their studio arguments offstage, they privately disagreed while publicly supporting the record. Mellencamp told *Creem* magazine that Ryder felt too much pressure about the project, thinking there was more at stake than just another album.

"I think he saw it as his one last break," Mellencamp said. "I don't see it that way at all; it's just another page in the Mitch Ryder story." Ryder was "never going away," Mellencamp said, and the body of work would weather the test of time.

The album didn't lack for promotion or expectations. *Detroit News* music writer Jim McFarlin pointed out the irony of Ryder being considered a "new artist" by the industry. "A legend's long night is breaking into dawn," McFarlin predicted. "The resurrected 38-year-old rock star is ready for the toughest part of his quest: showing he can still sock it to a concert audience."

In reverse fashion from the 1965 business Ryder entered, the album was recorded in its entirety before the first single was chosen. Polygram

Records spokesman Jeffrey Jaffe told Detroit's NBC affiliate WDIV—which aired a one-hour *For the Record* special on the recording and marketing of the album—that several songs were considered before the final decision was made.

It was a unanimous choice. The second track of the album stood out from the rest—a thumping bass-guitar line, a vocal performance that ranks among Ryder's all-time best, and a lyrical hook with an intriguing sense of word play: "I love you more than I did / When you were mine."

"We spent five days listening to it over and over," Jaffe said. It was the kind of song that grabs the listener with that indefinable "hook" sought by so many. "Once it gets into your head, you can't get it out. When something enters itself into your consciousness like that, it's a hit."

Not so fast, guys. This was 1983, not 1965, and a hit record was no longer the simple matter of putting a song on the radio and hoping people buy it. "When You Were Mine" wasn't considered ready-for-market until a short film was made for the fledgling cable television network that was now the proving ground for hit records, MTV—Music Television. "I want my MTV," American youths demanded—or so they were told by their television, which by the early 1980s was easily able to command such obedience.

Music Television hit the airwaves at midnight on August 1, 1981, with a video by British band the Buggles, the appropriately titled, "Video Killed the Radio Star." For those who appreciated the ability to create art through the playing of a musical instrument, Don McLean might have called MTV's launch, "The day the music died." A generational line was drawn between artists who developed their talent in basements, garages, or in front of audiences and those who perfected the ability to lip-sync in elaborate productions. (Incidentally, the Buggles were never heard from again.)

The video for "When You Were Mine" was directed by Laszlo Kovacs, a highly respected director of photography whose credits included *Easy Rider, Paper Moon,* and Martin Scorsese's landmark concert film, *The Last Waltz.* Kovacs was among the many Hollywood filmmakers eager to experiment with the strange new format—if nothing else, the finished product could be seen in weeks rather than the painstaking months or years before a full-length feature film was ready for viewing.

Kovacs was eager to use music videos to graduate from director of photography to a seat in the director's chair; he wasn't the only one with filmmaking ambitions. "John wanted Laszlo to direct the video to ease his own way into the Hollywood movie scene," Ryder said. In the multimedia-merging world of the 1980s, artistic pursuits were rarely restricted to a single enterprise. Actors made record albums; movies were turned into television shows and vice versa; and rock stars—as always—harbored ambitions of big-screen stardom. (In 1992 Mellencamp starred in a dramatic role in *Falling From Grace,* which he also directed. A bold choice. Unlike the typical pop star making a movie debut, Mellencamp did not portray a singer or frustrated singer in the Elvis Presley tradition but instead offered a tribute to his beloved Midwest farmlands.)

Although a veteran of both television and movie screen tests, Ryder said the world of video-making provided a new experience. "We went out to Los Angeles to make the video," Ryder said. "I'd never done an MTV thing; it was all Dick Clark or nothing, so that was kind of interesting."

Compared to the lavish productions they would quickly become, the video for "When You Were Mine" was a modest, two-day shoot. As with most of the vignettes, the videos were not simply a filmed performance of the song. MTV videos featured sometimes elaborate plots (or at least, the pretense thereof), some claiming to be mini-movies.

"It's a three-minute *Ben-Hur,*" Ryder told WDIV, tongue firmly in cheek. "An incredible video filled with bald-headed women and midgets." Kovacs' vision included something of a plot set in a Fellini-worthy strip club inspired more by the Moulin Rouge than the old 42nd Street venues. Ryder was featured in a story of sorts; his character woke up to the images of fantasy women while a surreal circus played in a nightclub. For music fans, the good news was that most of Ryder's screen time was spent performing the song on a stage set away from the weaving, indecipherable plotline.

"It was fun," Ryder said. "I was young enough not to be embarrassed by my physical appearance, so that didn't bother me. It was exciting to be part of that medium."

Without naming personalities, Ryder also recognized what hadn't changed in the business. "The slimy personalities hadn't left or vacated," he said. "The crooks and underworld creatures are still there. The good news is the technology is an enhancement of the music. The bad news is the incredible lack of morals and ethics."

Promotion of the *Sleeping Dog* album coexisted with the preparation of its material. Gone were the days when a product was put together and then sent off to market. Why do it that way—where fans can determine a record's quality—when you can spend months testing and marketing an album based on research and surveys that decide what "should"—not "could"—be a popular song?

Ryder was a busy man in the months leading up to the album's June 17 arrival in stores. In January, Mellencamp was sought by the American Music Awards for an appearance on the show and insisted that he be allowed to perform a duet with Ryder. The Midwest rockers belted out a version of "B.I.G. T.I.M.E." from the *Sleeping Dog* album, a trade-off for Mellencamp's performance of "Ain't Even Done with the Night." An interesting pairing of voices: outsiders, loners with a soul, white boys more comfortable with black intonations than with sugar-coated pop; awkward yet passionate dancers. As much as James Brown and Little Richard once influenced Ryder, it was obvious how much inspiration Ryder had given Mellencamp.

Approaching the release date, Ryder held nothing back in his promotion for the product. The challenge was to get airplay on radio, which—in spite of MTV's increasing importance—was still the key element needed to attract buyers to record stores.

That much was the same, but the competitive nature of the business increased dramatically from previous decades. Even with a familiar name on the album cover, the odds were heavily against success. Bill Thom, manager of record store chain Harmony House, said 97 percent of the dozens of albums received each week failed to remain a part of the store inventory before being sent back to the warehouse. "For seven dollars, people won't take a chance on something they haven't heard before,"

Ryder with John Mellencamp at the 1983 American Music Awards. Rising star Mellencamp produced Ryder's *Never Kick a Sleeping Dog* album that returned the singer to the national spotlight. (Photo by Robert Matheu.)

Thom said. Few industries challenge their product suppliers with a 97 percent failure rate.

Ryder banged the drum, loudly, touring the country to visit radio stations, give interviews, and promote the album. It had been nearly a year since Mellencamp casually mentioned his admiration for Ryder while in Detroit, and in the summer of 1983 the fate of the album was in the hands of the record-buying public.

Was Ryder's name enough? Detroit disc jockeys including Doug Podell of WLLZ and WABX's Paul Christy predicted the album would probably reach the 30s or 40s on the Billboard charts; its single, "When You Were Mine," was a potential Top Ten candidate in the minds of veteran radio personalities.

The reality fell short of those goals. *Never Kick a Sleeping Dog* first appeared on the *Billboard* sales charts on July 16 at No. 182, and reached No. 121 at its peak. "When You Were Mine" entered the charts at No. 95 and never climbed above No. 85. The album sold nearly 80,000 early copies, more than respectable numbers for a newcomer but a disappointment for a veteran.

Maybe there wasn't enough dancing, in either the video or the lyrics. Although the top single during the summer of 1983 was "Every Breath You Take"—an oddly romantic ballad of stalking by British trio the Police—MTV's influence was evident in just about every other song released that year. Rather than simply inspire people to move their feet and shake it up, baby, music was often about dancing itself, notably seen in the hit movie *Flashdance,* a Cinderella story about a factory worker who becomes a ballerina (happens all the time). Irene Cara's title song, "What a Feeling," was a runaway hit on radio and MTV, as was the bottomless pit of singles from Michael Jackson's milestone album, *Thriller,* including "Billie Jean" and "Beat It," songs known more for the video images of Jackson's considerable dance talents than for the rhythm or lyrics. Veteran rocker David Bowie joined the club with "Let's Dance," and the last strains of disco echoed from Donna Summer's ode to a prostitute, "She Works Hard for the Money," a vocal performance convincing enough to give birth to urban legends that the singer previously worked the lady-of-the-evening trade. (She didn't.)

Clearly the music of the early 1980s wasn't feeding the same appetite felt a generation earlier, when albums were listened to (rather than seen) in their entirety, and lyrics required thought to fully grasp their meaning. Regardless of the quality of *Never Kick a Sleeping Dog,* classic rhythm and blues or straight-out rock and roll seemed almost anachronistic in an era of Madonna, Boy George, and music that was meant to be viewed more than heard.

The album was further handicapped by backstage business problems. Both the album and video exceeded Polygram's proposed budget, and the company decided not to exercise its option for a second album. Ryder was, again, a man without a label. "A lot of people thought it would go further than it did," Ryder said.

The experience was not without rewards—with a record being heard on American radio and concert performances that allowed Ryder to do what he did best. Overall, he was reminded of the nature of celebrity in a nation of disposable appetites.

"The funniest part to me was watching the people," Ryder said. "The higher the record would go on the charts, the prettier the women would get. It's just so American. Fame never really changed; it's just more frequent and more people want it, even if it means degrading themselves on television. It's a disease in this country."

The partnership with Mellencamp was a one-time only collaboration. Ryder proved he could hold his own alongside music's Young Turks. Mellencamp remained enough of a Ryder fan to include the influential name in his salute, "R.O.C.K. in the U.S.A.," from the 1986 album *Scarecrow*: "There was Frankie Lymon, Bobby Fuller, Mitch Ryder (they were rockin'); Jackie Wilson, Shangri-Las, Young Rascals (they were rockin'), Spotlight on Martha Reeves and don't forget James Brown."

Pretty good company, on the whole. Rockin' in the U.S.A.

The author of "When You Were Mine" was a multitalented singer, guitarist, and performer from Minneapolis, who (as with Madonna) used only one of his three names, Prince Rogers Nelson. A blues-based, jazz-inspired musician, Prince first claimed mainstream success with the 1982 album *1999*, which included the title song and the hit single, "Delirious." As capable of pushing for new musical frontiers as he was composing catchy tunes, Prince's "Little Red Corvette" competed for chart space in late 1983 with Ryder's "When You Were Mine." The following year would witness his biggest commercial success, with the album and film *Purple Rain*.

During a 1983 concert by Prince at Detroit's Cobo Hall, Ryder was invited to see the show, perhaps meet the young star. The performance included a rendition of "When You Were Mine" that deviated from Prince's original version in favor of the arrangement crafted by Ryder and Mellencamp, likely a nod to the hometown hero in the audience. "He apparently knew where I was seated and looked up at me during the performance,"

Ryder said. "I was invited to go backstage and meet Prince."

Ryder was escorted down a longer corridor than he knew existed at Cobo, "an endless, cavernous hall so far removed from the stage I couldn't believe it," Ryder said. His escort, a gentleman of sufficient size that Ryder called him "more animal than man," knocked on a dressing-room door that stood slightly ajar. "Mitch Ryder," the escort announced before leaving. Ryder stood alone in the silent hall before a half-open door.

"I didn't know if I should walk in or not," Ryder said. "I stuck my head in the door, said, 'Prince?' He was sitting down at the other end of the room in front of a mirror, all the lights on, just looking at himself." An awkward moment: Prince stared at Ryder—seen in the lightbulb-framed mirror—for up to a full minute without speaking. "I was waiting for something to be said, and nothing was said," Ryder recalled. "He broke his eyes away from me, went back to looking at himself." Ryder complimented the performer on his show, closed the door, and walked out.

They never actually spoke, but Ryder heard there was some resentment from members of the Prince camp, a tired old argument he grew weary of in the 1960s. In short: White men had no business singing a black man's blues. A pitiful accusation at this stage of Ryder's career. Before Prince ever picked up his first guitar, Ryder was respected by—and friends with—artists including Jimi Hendrix, Otis Redding, Wilson Pickett, and James Brown, who told Johnny Carson that Ryder had the best blues voice of any white man in the game. Race-based criticisms from those who enjoyed the fame and wealth made possible by the true black pioneers—who suffered the type of racism and resentment that Prince and his contemporaries could only read about in history books—was as offensive as it was inappropriate.

Especially insulting was that the negative comments came not so much from Prince but from the assorted hangers-on in the musician's Minnesota-based company. "They gave him [Prince] a lecture about Mitch Ryder being just another white boy trying to rip off the black man," Ryder said. "When I was growing up, it wasn't a question of ripping off anybody. I was deeply immersed in black culture, sang in black groups, and was familiar with the lifestyle and the culture." Ryder had more than paid his dues, and the fortunes Prince would receive from audiences—both black and white—were made possible by musicians who looked beyond race before and leading up to the civil rights movement, experiments in social equality that included Ryder's days of singing with the black trio, the Peps.

In the years to follow, a public debate was briefly heard in song lyrics. For his 1994 album *Rite of Passage,* Ryder composed a piece called "It Wasn't Me" with less than subtle lyrics: "Somebody stole the prince's royal pass, it wasn't me." The recording was reportedly heard by Prince, who answered the charge on a video where dancers were heard singing, "Devil with a Blue Dress." A public feud over a private misunderstanding.

"I got him; he hit me back," Ryder said. "It's similar to what happened between Lynyrd Skynyrd and Neil Young." The veteran rockers clashed over Young's "Southern Man," which Skynyrd took personally, responding that the southern man, "Don't need him around, anyhow" in their homespun tribute, "Sweet Home Alabama."

"That's how we talk to each other as artists," Ryder said.

Once a member of a group—a rock-and-roll band—always a member. The four Beatles spent the 1970s deflecting offers to reunite; Paul Simon and Art Garfunkel are rarely interviewed without being asked about a reunion. The Eagles, the Who, and countless other musicians are forever linked to the sounds that made them famous. (Perhaps the only exception to this rule is the curious case of the Rolling Stones; are Mick Jagger and Keith Richards *ever* going to end their nearly fifty-year partnership?)

In the wake of the *Sleeping Dog* album and its failure to secure an American album contract, Ryder accepted the inevitable and teamed again with guitarist Jim McCarty and drummer Johnny Badanjek. Was there room for a reunited Detroit Wheels in the MTV-dictated world of rock music in the mid-1980s?

The three veterans, approaching their fortieth birthdays, agreed to a series of concerts, the description of which Ryder phrased carefully for a July, 1984, profile in the *Detroit News*. "The key word is *reunion*," Ryder said, leaving no doubt as to the limited expectations for the tour.

As with the brief 1978 show, longtime fans—especially those in the Detroit area—understood the difference in having McCarty and Badanjek join Ryder on stage. For fans in America, it was nostalgia. In Europe, Ryder and the Wheels did a two-week run before fans that barely knew of McCarty and Badanjek's now defunct band, the Rockets, but were well versed in Ryder's post-1977 material. The brief tour included a few hometown shows at the familiar stage of Pine Knob. "It's like a family reunion," Ryder said, "Where you go and have a big party, and when the picnic's over, you don't go back home together."

Unlike the 1978 reunion, Ryder's *Sleeping Dog* exposure left little doubt in the minds of music writers as to the motivations held by the players. "Ryder needed a push," McFarlin wrote. "The ex-Rockets needed a gig."

There were high expectations though. Plans were made for a mini-LP's worth of Wheels music, to be produced by Bob Ezrin with help from the increasingly powerful Don Was. The eighteen-song Pine Knob concerts were recorded both on audio- and videotape by Capitol Records, shows that began with Ryder's rendition of the Don Was party tune, "Bow Wow Wow Wow," included the Wheels' now-classic hits and demonstrated a diverse range that surprised some fans.

In a *Detroit News* review, McFarlin called the show: "A textbook example of what Detroit rock and roll is supposed to be. Rampaging, relentless, vital, a pure gut-busting sonic celebration." For a welcome change, the best-received material was not "Devil with a Blue Dress On" or "Jenny Take a Ride"; it was the singer, with a scream to match Wilson Pickett's and a blistering version of "Gimme Shelter" that moved the crowd.

The stage show was a curious mix of where Ryder had been and where he might be going: McCarty and Badanjek represented, "the old Wheels," an affectionate description offered by guitarist Robert Gillespie, who in 1983 began a working relationship with Ryder that lasted—off and on—into the next century. A product of Detroit about a decade behind Ryder and the original Wheels, Gillespie's twelve-year-old ears perked up to the

Jim McCarty and Ryder during the 1984 Detroit Wheels reunion at Pine Knob, an outdoor venue north of Detroit. (Photo by Robert Alford.)

1966 sounds of "Jenny Take a Ride" when it dominated local airplay. A garage band was formed in high school, the Wise Guys, which wasn't destined for longevity. "I think we had one gig," Gillespie said. "I made my first record when I was eighteen years old, all about the [right of people our age to] vote, called "You've Got the Power."

Gillespie joined the next generation of Detroit's rock scene, becoming familiar with the players and personalities. In the late 1970s, he joined with Rob Tyner for a recast edition of the MC5, and ran in similar circles that Ryder traveled. They discussed working together after meeting in the fall of 1977, a conversation that was renewed after "When You Were Mine" was released in 1983.

"I heard that song and thought it was just great," Gillespie said. Although written as a statement of lost love, Gillespie's familiarity with Ryder's career heard a separate meaning in the lyrics: "It was like he was talking to the audience," Gillespie said. "'When you were mine.' It was a great song. I loved it and just had to have that gig."

For Gillespie, the opportunities represented a dramatic promotion from where he had been working and playing. "That was a very good year," Gillespie said. "I had a ball on the road then, becoming an international guy. We went all over America, to Europe, Japan, everywhere. It was fun . . . big fun. Once you've had that taste, you really want to work to achieve that again."

Between the release of *Never Kick a Sleeping Dog* and the Pine Knob reunion concert, the Mitch Ryder show enjoyed the broader spotlight that comes with a product in record stores, a single on the radio and a video on MTV. They opened for the Little River Band during a three-night engagement at the Universal Amphitheater in Los Angeles and shared bills with that year's top acts, including Cheap Trick and Eddie Money. "Those were a lot of fun; real good gigs," Gillespie said. "Big clubs, packed houses, arenas. It was a great time."

The Pine Knob Wheels reunion show was among the last American shows before Ryder went back to Europe. For Gillespie, playing alongside original bandsmen McCarty and Badanjek represented certification of a Detroit rocker made good.

"It was a real treat," said Gillespie, who held a guitarist's respect for McCarty's work and a musician's estimation that Badanjek was the perfect drummer to back Ryder's voice. "It was just so weird, after all those years; here I am onstage with those guys."

But a summer night's concert did not a career—or a living—make. Capitol Records shelved the recordings made of the shows, and Ryder and the original Wheels took their bows and sought their fortunes elsewhere. After two years of pushing for American exposure, Ryder plunged

Flanked by Jim McCarty (*left*) and Robert Gillespie, Ryder headlined the "Guitar Army" tour of 1985. (Photo by Robert Alford.)

headlong back to Europe; the Rockpalast audiences remained receptive of new material.

"Over there, I can write and sing and it's accepted on its own merits," Ryder said. "I don't have all these thirty- or forty-year-olds asking, 'What happened to Mitch Ryder?'"

In the second half of the Eighties, Ryder released a steady flow of albums, including the *Legendary Full Moon Concert*, the 1986 release *In the*

China Shop, and a compilation album for his European fans, *Red Blood, White Mink,* that avoided "Jenny Take a Ride" and "Devil with a Blue Dress On" in favor of a broader retrospective.

A departure for Ryder came with a limited-release single in 1987, "Good Golly, Ask Ollie," a political parody making use of one of Ryder's signature phrases to address a United States Marine colonel whose (non)testimony during the Iran-Contra hearings betrayed the perception of what *honor* could or should mean. Oliver North stubbornly held his oath to defend his commander in chief, President Ronald Reagan, and stood silent against the charges at hand: that the United States had illegally sold arms to Iran as a means of funding "freedom fighters" in Nicaragua, an agreement that dated back to the 1979 hostage crisis in Iran. As with all complicated stories of intrigue, North's testimony inspired mixed responses. Some claimed North was "taking the fall" for Reagan; others felt he betrayed his country. North was convicted of the presented charges, a decision later overturned on appeal.

"Good Golly, Ask Ollie" was an inspired bit of lunacy produced by Mark Black, featuring Paul Schaeffer, the bandleader Ryder met during a 1983 appearance on *The David Letterman Show.* "[Schafer] was responsible for getting me on *Letterman,*" Ryder said.

At the time, Ryder was promoting a dance single produced by Don Was, a rhythmic version of Bob Dylan's "Like a Rolling Stone." The idea of a "tribute" to Oliver North was born of Ryder's fascination with the Marine's dedication to a false ideal and belief that the testimony (or sometimes, nontestimony) concealed crimes committed in a higher office.

"I was entranced by the testimony given in Congress," Ryder said. "North was relentlessly defending Reagan, when all along [it seemed obvious that] Reagan was guilty, and here was a soldier willing to go to the firing squad."

Unlike a previous generation, the revelations from the scandal did not inspire outrage, protest, or rebellion from America's youth. Although some musicians were socially active (including Irish singer Bob Geldof, whose humanitarian efforts culminated in the *Live Aid* concerts to provide famine relief to a desperately struggling Africa), political protest was

Ryder with producer Don Was. (Photo courtesy of Mitch Ryder.)

more often the playground of comedians than musicians. North was lampooned on such vehicles as *Saturday Night Live* (with *Star Trek* actor William Shatner backed by a "Ballad of the Green Berets" spoof, "The Mute Marine"), but few from the MTV generation chose protest over popularity. In many ways, everyone was in on the joke: Colonel North was photographed, smiling, holding a copy of the "Ask Ollie" single. (Kudos to the colonel for having a sense of humor; no comment on the apathy of Americans.)

It wasn't always funny. The 1980s came to end with more to celebrate in Germany than in North America; the 1989 fall of the Berlin Wall brought an ugly period of European history to an end. In a less danceable mode, Ryder wrote a song early in the decade, "Er Ist Nicht Mein President" ("He is not my president"), concerned with the highly questionable Reagan administration but also with what might be in store under a possible presidency of George H. W. Bush.

In the late 1980s Ryder's band included (*left to right*) Billy Csernits, Robert Gillespie, Mitch Ryder, Mark Gougeon, John Badanjek, and Joe Gutz. (Photo courtesy of Mitch Ryder.)

Maybe the rock stars were tired, weary of a business that offered few new adventures and presented little in the way of challenges to be conquered. Away from the American spotlight, Ryder spent time with other veterans. Dr. Hook—who scored a novelty hit in 1972, the Shel Silverstein-penned "Cover of the *Rolling Stone*"—spent a drinker's evening with Ryder in an Amsterdam club. The boredom of life on the road was evident in their choice of additional companions.

At the Second Chance during a 1987 show. Ryder was familiar with the Ann Arbor club, having made his first appearance there since leaving the business in 1979. (Photo by Robert Alford.)

"We sat in a bar one night and decided we needed more company," Ryder said. "We went outside to a flatbed truck, took a big old truck tire, brought it back in, sat it on a fucking chair, and bought drinks for it."

He met heroes—James Brown, Little Richard—and sometimes played with them. Ryder shared stories with the next generation of stars, including Freddie Mercury, whose band Queen also lost favor in American while remaining major stars elsewhere. Behind the curtains, away from the spotlight, the musicians found common ground.

"He was angry about something," Ryder recalled his ships-passing-in-the-night encounter with Mercury. "But there was no pretense. Maybe because I was a fellow musician he didn't have any concerns about displaying his emotions publicly."

It's not a happy picture Ryder described, the years (even decades) on the road catching up to the players. "Lonely for companionship, like every bar I've ever been to," is the image Ryder paints. (With humor, though. Ryder was of a generation able to appreciate the irony of British Invasion musicians and their followers having to make a name for themselves elsewhere in Europe. "The British always go there; it's fate that leaves them stranded in Germany," Ryder said. "They gotta do time in the country that almost bombed them off the fucking map.")

Ryder wondered if he was destined to remain a performer in Europe and a nostalgia act in his own country. The same drink-drug-excess cloud that was cast over the band Detroit was repeating itself on another continent, in another decade. "Very negative and destructive," Ryder said of the lifestyle he lived. "Why was I destroying myself? Was it bitterness because I didn't have an American market? The question crossed my mind, but that wasn't really the reason."

Yet another new decade lay ahead. Would Ryder be more comfortable at home, in Europe, or perhaps a combination of the best of both worlds?

CHAPTER TEN

CLASSIC ROCK

Most people would have probably wanted to wash their hands. Not Mitch Ryder.

"Now I'm going to go to a massage parlor," joked the forty-four-year-old Ryder, adjusting his now ever-present Ray-Bans as four hundred fans gathered in Royal Oak, Michigan. Ryder had just plunged his hands into wet cement outside of the Metropolitan Music Café: the first block of cement for the Michigan "Rock Walk of Fame," a tribute to the state's music talent. In March 1999, Ryder's were the first handprints immortalized at the suburban nightclub, a carved-in-cement exhibit cosponsored by WRIF-FM ("the undisputable home of kick-ass rock and roll . . . Baby!" in the words of disc jockey Arthur Penhallow).

For Ryder and his contemporaries, the early 1990s marked a transitional period, caught between nostalgia for the songs of the past and the desire to continue their growth as artists. Tributes were all well and good—flattering, without a doubt—but a living still had to be earned. Eu-

At a Detroit Chamber of Commerce event at Greenfield Village with hockey legend Gordie Howe and Michigan governor Jennifer Granholm. (Photo courtesy of Mitch Ryder.)

ropean album releases from Ryder continued at a steady pace, including the 1990 compilation *The Beautiful Toulang Sunset* and the 1992 release, *La Gash,* a "concept" album of sorts exploring the theme of relationships. Ryder toured in America frequently, but his enjoyment struggled against the toll of travel; a musical road with a destination seen more in the rearview mirror than what may lie ahead.

In the Detroit area—and every other market in the country—long-standing rock-and-roll radio stations became categorized. The prominent stations, including WRIF, shared space on the dial with what used to be called "oldies" stations, now preferring the haughtier term "classic rock." Leading the Detroit menu in this format was WCSX, with a lineup of on-air personalities drafted from jockeys previously employed by the upstart FM stations of the 1970s. The rock-and-roll generation was approaching middle age, and listening habits followed suit. ("We used to look for killer weed," quipped WCSX's Jim Johnson. "Now we just want a good weed killer.") Those who once prowled Woodward Avenue in search of rowdy good times settled into the suburban pursuit of a quiet Sunday afternoon. Radio executives recognized the need to deliver programming that was hip, yet comfortable. Like a perfectly worn and faded pair of blue jeans . . . provided they still fit.

Mitch Ryder's Radio Playhouse was conceived by WCSX programmers Mark Passman and Tom Dalton; a weekly talk-and-tune show with an ear toward nostalgia. For Ryder, the trip down memory lane included appreciation for the show's less-than-desirable time slot.

"There was a part of me that was old enough to remember when radio was the Sunday evening entertainment," said Ryder, born before television sets dominated living rooms and gathering around the old Philco brought the world into your home. Once upon a time, radio offered "an entertaining, friendly voice on the other end," Ryder said. "It was like having a friend talking to you while you were doing your chores. It wasn't beyond my imagination that I would be able to capture some people."

In the 1990s, however, the Sunday evening time slot was not quite as attractive. "Yeah, there wasn't going to be much of an audience base for it," Ryder sighed.

The format for *Playhouse* was straightforward: Guests joined Ryder for a few hours on the radio, not so much to promote new products (movies, television shows, or records) as to have a conversation with someone who understood American celebrity. Ryder's radio show expanded beyond music to include some memorable guests.

"I not only talked to Mr. Rogers, but he was nice enough to go into character on the air," Ryder said of fond memories of children's television host Fred Rogers. "We talked about his motivations, his beginnings." Rogers, a very spiritual man in his private life, practiced perhaps the purest form of religion, one that didn't insist that he promote his beliefs to others. The education of children—in his timeless, gentle style—was his focus, one that was among the most successful in television history.

"He was very steeped in his religion," Ryder said. "We skirted around that; he didn't want to jam that down anyone's throats. It was wonderful. He was just a very nice man."

Mitch Ryder's Radio Playhouse aired for two years and produced more

Publicity still, early 1990s. "My Conway Twitty period," Ryder called the look. (Photo courtesy of Mitch Ryder.)

than one hundred shows. The program nearly failed during its debut broadcast. The very first scheduled guest was a local television anchor who battled a number of personal struggles that were beginning to interfere with his work.

"He called the night of the show to say he wouldn't be there," Ryder said. "He just couldn't make it." The newscaster was more than a little inebriated when he called Ryder, now facing a three-hour time slot of talking in which he would be be talking to himself.

Desperate, Ryder called Bob Talbert, a longtime friend and veteran *Detroit Free Press* columnist. "I was frantic," Ryder laughed. "I said, 'Bob, what am I gonna do?'" Talbert contacted the reluctant guest with a simple proposition: If you don't do the show, you're going to read about it in tomorrow's *Free Press.*

"So he showed up," Ryder said of the successful blackmail. "He had this old whore with him. Her tits were falling out of her too-tight dress; both of their wigs were slightly askew. He did the interview. It was a great show."

Air time on the radio (as with newspaper column inches and television time slots) has an insatiable appetite. Certainly Ryder was able to call upon a host of musical and notable guests, but the broadcast booth's ON THE AIR sign constantly demanded more. On two occasions, Ryder enlisted his wife, Margaret, to play a radio psychologist, with call-in guests seeking answers to personal problems. "She brought advice to people who called in with serious problems," Ryder laughed. "I'm not sure it was healthy—or legal—but it was fun; it was what radio used to be."

Of course, music was at the heart of the *Playhouse,* and shows often featured a particular artist, with guest stars ranging from Bonnie Raitt to an old acquaintance of Ryder's from his Greenwich Village days a quarter century earlier, Bo Diddley. "He didn't really want to take the call," Ryder said. "But because it was me he said okay." The phone was answered by 'Bo Diddley's man,' a valet/assistant who, Ryder said, identified himself as such: "Bo Diddley's Man."

At the time of the call, Diddley was working on the engine of an old car, and "Bo Diddley's Man" held the telephone to the ear of the guitar leg-

At the Motor City Music Awards in May 1994 with Bob Seger and George Clinton. (Photo courtesy of Mitch Ryder.)

end. It was not a very focused interview. "When he dropped something or scraped his knuckle, you'd hear the curse words come out," Ryder said. "The car hadn't run in a long time; he described the weeds coming up through the bottom of the engine. That's how we conducted the interview."

It was an interesting two-year run, but Ryder's performance schedule and recording commitments in Europe prevented him from fulfilling the live interview portion of his contract. A mutual parting of the ways brought to an end a show that allowed Ryder to expand his boundaries into comedy, conversation, and the acting he had once tried.

"I brought in other people; we did voices. My neighbor had a funny voice, and he became a 'Representative' from the state," Ryder said. "It was fun, it was comedy, and nobody was real. Sometimes I wondered if I was."

Although his music isn't typically mentioned in the annals of political rock—songs with a social agenda or statement to be made—Ryder occasionally stepped on stages more issue driven than entertainment oriented. In the first half of the 1980s, Ryder was briefly linked to a death penalty debate in Michigan. Oakland County's feisty, fiery prosecutor, Republican L. Brooks Patterson, launched a 1982 gubernatorial campaign and embraced as one of his issues the reinstatement of the death penalty. Patterson successfully placed a ballot question for the August primary election to bring capital punishment back to Michigan. Democratic candidate Zolton Ferency challenged the referendum, with help from a celebrity friend. (Neither Patterson nor Ferency won their party's nomination during the primary election.)

Ryder's name was attached to the lawsuit filed by Ferency, prompted in part by his friendship with the lawyer handling the case, flamboyant, driven attorney Geoffrey Fieger. (Music fans interested in trivia should note that Fieger's brother, Doug, was the lead singer of the Knack, which scored a No. 1 hit in 1979 with "My Sharona.")

Fieger and Ryder opposed Patterson's version of a reinstated death penalty, which would have allowed for accomplices in murder cases to be executed. Although Ferency, in theory, was the lawsuit's lead plaintiff, the *Detroit Free Press* eagerly quoted the more recognizable name. Celebrity rules, even in matters of legal challenges and politics.

"If we're going to go, 'Eye for an eye,' why don't we just have the relatives of the victim take the life of the murderer," Ryder said at a July 1982 press conference. "The death penalty is wrong, and I don't think the state should take the role of sponsoring it." The ballot question failed to gain voter support but resurfaced periodically more as a campaign issue than a serious movement, a passion that seemed strongest among its advocates—as with many other issues—during even-numbered years.

Ryder may have assumed that political causes being championed from the world of rock and roll remained what they were in the late 1960s, when few bands did not include social beliefs in their lyrics. In the 1990s, however, Ryder learned the hard way that even former radical liberals were nervous about rocking uncertain boats. That was made obvious when he struck up a friendship—through Fieger—with Michigan's controversial advocate of assisted suicide, Dr. Jack Kevorkian.

In 1994, another ballot issue was put before Michigan voters, this one contesting state laws that prohibited doctors from helping terminal patients end their suffering. Unlike the 1982 death penalty campaign (in which Ryder played at best a peripheral role), Ryder was an active participant in Kevorkian's organization, (Movement Ensuring the Right to Choose for Yourself). Ryder composed a song titled, "Mercy," for the 1994 album, *Rite of Passage.* The *Detroit News* reported on March 22 that proceeds from sales of the song would go to Kevorkian's campaign. Its lyrics began:

Cast your spell, Dr. Jack;
I am willing, I can't wait;
End my pain/no one else,
Seems to understand my fate.

In a true revelation of the period's priorities, the *Free Press* asked Ryder if a music video would be made for "Mercy," which obviously wasn't in the plans. "I can only imagine what *that* would look like," Ryder said.

Since 1990, Kevorkian had watched (and assisted) as more than twenty patients ended their lives, and his beliefs became a topic of national debate. Unlike a previous generation's willingness to ally themselves with causes that might be controversial, people in the 1990s were less eager to take part in such a campaign.

In August, Ryder's support for Kevorkian prompted a decision by John Hertel, general manager of the Michigan State Fair, that Ryder's scheduled performance at the annual event not include any "new" songs. Ryder called the decision what it was—censorship—and canceled the show. "I find it impossible to perform under these conditions," Ryder said.

Hertel said the ban was not specific to the song "Mercy" but rather that Ryder was hired as "an oldies act," under the condition that he not perform any new songs. "The only reason we wanted him was to sing oldies," Hertel said. "I said that I didn't want this song ["Mercy"] or any new song." Ryder was replaced on the State Fair stage by another oldies act, Steppenwolf, who performed their hippie-era hits, including "Magic Carpet Ride," a rocking salute to drug-inspired hallucinations; it was good of the State Fair people to keep the show family friendly.

Members of the State Fair board weren't the only ones nervous about "Mercy," Dr. Jack, or anything else that might bring controversy. Things had changed, ever so much, since the early 1970s. Within weeks of the shootings at Kent State University, rocker Neil Young enlisted the help of partners David Crosby, Stephen Stills, and Graham Nash for a rush recording of "Ohio," a song that pulled no punches in its political accusations.

However, such controversial attitudes were no longer acceptable, and not just by conservative, right-wing Republicans. "Don't take a chance. Don't frighten the kids," Ryder commented. "We have this imaginary view that we hold of our ideals; it's hypocritical."

The winds of change were first felt in the mid-1980s, when middle-aged liberals were worried that their children might be doing the same things they themselves had done at a younger age. A group called the Parents Music Resource Center—led by Tipper Gore, the wife of Senator (and future Vice President) Al Gore—campaigned against what they called "porn rock." These guardians of decency realized that (gasp!) some popular music included lyrics of a sexually suggestive nature. (That never, of course, happened in the 1960s.) A campaign was launched—but it was fought against by an odd collection of musical comrades including the always intellectual Frank Zappa, Dee Snyder of the heavily made-up Twisted Sister, and country-pop nice guy John Denver. The goal of the PMRC was to have albums and CDs that included suggestive lyrics identified as such; a "parental warning label" on the cover, based on the obviously flawed presumption that moms and dads went record shopping with their teenage children. The legislation did not, however, include a provision preventing retailers from selling the offensive material to anyone under eighteen. The campaign's primary accomplishment was the increased sale of CDs by artists who would have otherwise likely faded into obscurity.

By the time Ryder participated in the complicated issue of assisted suicide, few allies were found, even among liberals, record companies or radio program directors. "I wrote the song in support of the idea of assisted suicide," Ryder said. "Unfortunately people mistook that to mean that I condoned Jack's exact philosophy. I wrote it, sincerely, because I was friends with Jack and felt it was imperative that people who are terminally ill have the dignity to exit when they want. Geoffrey [Fieger], of course, jumped all over it."

The song "Mercy" was, at best, a footnote in the Kevorkian saga, but the political climate of the mid-1990s, in spite of the most progressively liberal president since Kennedy, was not favorable to radical ideas. The counterculture had become mainstream, and for every pretense of tolerance there was an equal inclination toward conservative thought. As with his European releases, Ryder was unable to find air time on American radio stations, most of which were no longer independent but were part of a network controlled by corporate determinations.

"Before looking for an American deal, we sent it around to all these radio stations just to get their opinions," Ryder said, believing that "Mercy" was the root of the problem. "Not one of them responded. Why? Because of the attention given to one song."

It was an interesting contrast. If someone had told an FM disc jockey in 1972 that a particular record might be "controversial," little time would have been wasted in putting the needle to the vinyl. Political and social controversies in the 1990s, however, were more about personality than about substantive issues. A president was nearly impeached over personal, not criminal, behavior. The murder trial of O. J. Simpson was around-the-clock headline news for its celebrity value, its verdict linked by many historians to the ugly racism revealed by the 1992 acquittal of Los Angeles police officers for the brutality against Rodney King, a beating not seen since the early 1960s South.

Kevorkian continued to push the legislative envelope. A December 1994 ruling by the Michigan Supreme Court upheld the state's ban on assisted suicide, allowing for the reinstatement of charges against Kevorkian, who appeared at a Pontiac courthouse in 1995 wearing a homemade stock and ball-and-chain. He opened a Springfield Township "suicide clinic," further dividing public opinion. In November 1998, Kevorkian was seen on CBS's *60 Minutes* administering a lethal injection to a patient suffering from Lou Gehrig's disease. In April 1999, the seventy-year-old Kevorkian was found guilty of second-degree murder, and sentenced to ten to twenty-five years in prison. (Due to his failing health, Kevorkian was released in June 2007.)

It was a tangled, drawn-out affair, and Kevorkian remained stubborn to his cause, even against the legal advice given by Fieger. "Geoffrey told him he couldn't keep him out of jail if he kept doing these things," Ryder said. "But Jack wouldn't listen."

After the *Rite of Passage* turmoil, Ryder took a break and waited until 1999 to release what he considered his best work to date, *Monkey Island*. The album, produced by "Good Golly, Ask Ollie" producer Mark Black, was an experimental project in many ways. "Some guys in a New York studio created this weird, grating, industrial music," Ryder said. "They wanted me to do some words and melodies."

Maybe it was his age that made the job challenging; perhaps it was the expected reaction of an artist trained in the finer points of music to the nonhuman sounds coming from "electronic" music—a hybrid descendant of synthesizers and digital loops that removed the human element of playing a musical instrument. (The concept reflected the coming wave of "electronic music" that would become its own subgenre, a category of sound born in Detroit.)

In time, Ryder felt he understood the sound well enough to put words to its rhythms, melodies to its programmed beats. "The level of creativity that was required was the highest that has even been demanded of me," Ryder said. "At first, honest to God, I couldn't listen to fifteen seconds of it. This went on for a couple of weeks."

Out of friendship, an obligation of promise, Ryder did what he always had and fulfilled his professional commitment. "I adjusted my sights, trained my ears, and began finding that there were places for me to enter and involve myself," Ryder said. "We created a beast. I worked harder on that album than any other album in my life."

No small statement. By the time America stopped holding its breath that "Y2K" would signal the end of humanity (or, worse, its now-essential computers), Ryder had put his name on twenty-two record albums from which dozens of singles had been released. A conservative estimate of live performances counts more than eight thousand shows he performed. He appeared on nearly every television show that carried rock and roll in the 1960s, and room was made in subsequent decades for appearances on *The David Letterman Show* and a revised version of *Hollywood Squares*.

In spite of not having new record releases, Ryder remained a popular stage act, either for profit or purpose. In the 1960s, Ryder participated in antiwar demonstrations—a cause he believed in—while also performing in USO shows for troops at American military bases, support he equally felt a passion for. ("You can honor and support our warriors, but you don't have to support their mission," Ryder once said, a statement as true in 1967 as in 2006.) At the height of his fame he was the national spokesman for the American Heart Association (although they asked him, please, not to smoke while performing benefits for the worthy organization), and on Detroit television stations rare was the fund-raising telethon or event that didn't include Ryder's participation.

He continued doing benefit concerts, some with unplanned comedic results. Ryder was doing a charity performance in Port Huron, a coastal town in Michigan's "Thumb" region. The show was going well, Ryder outfitted in complete rock-and-roll regalia to include his now-trademark sunglasses. Tossing Frisbees into the crowd seemed a good idea during an instrumental jam, and Ryder hurled the first disc into the audience. He heard a *thunk* sound, and the voice of someone yelling out. Another Frisbee was sent from the singer's hand into the audience; another *thunk* and vocal reaction. Someone rushed from the side of the stage to remind Ryder that he was performing at a benefit for the visually impaired— and was throwing Frisbees at blind people.

Some concerts were memorable more in hindsight than what at the time seemed to be just another gig. Writer Jay Burstein enjoyed a lunch-hour concert Ryder gave in New York City in 2001. Burstein said it was perhaps the tenth time he had seen Ryder perform over the years, yet the show matched the intensity of the twenty-year-old performer from the past. "The singer emoted a seemingly inexhaustible amount of energy and passion in each and every song over the course of the two-hour concert," Burstein wrote.

The show was part of a summer lunchtime series held in the courtyard between the twin towers of the World Trade Center. Ryder's show on August 28 was the last concert played at that location, two weeks before the terrorist attacks of September 11, 2001.

"I'm just going to talk through the songs," Ryder told the four musicians standing before him. No big deal, he implied; no need to work too hard.

It was an informal rehearsal for a one-time only performance, at which Ryder was backed by a group of semiprofessional players. They were more than capable, he knew, of learning the relatively simple arrangements for a dozen or so classic songs he'd performed thousands of times. For the rehearsal run-through, there was no need to do anything more than "just talk through" the familiar lyrics.

That was the intention, at any rate. The songs (including "Jenny Take a Ride" and "Devil with a Blue Dress On") were nearly as familiar to the band as to the singer. The musicians were a basement-born, Detroit-area band, and Ryder was among the heroes who inspired their musical aspirations.

The keyboard sounded the opening chords to "Jenny," a crawling bass line rumbled alongside a steady backbeat on the drums, a guitar slapped out complimentary chords in sync with the piano, and Ryder began "talking" his way through the lyrics. Ryder issued the first line. The tempo took hold; the beat filled the room. Ryder rocked slightly, his head nodding in time while he mentally danced to the tune. He grabbed the microphone with one hand, the other punching the air in time to the music, conducting a four-man orchestra with the precision of a concert maestro.

Ryder had lied. He couldn't just "talk his way" through the songs, even after all these years. Within a few words—a line of lyrics memorized long before by twenty-year-old William Levise Jr. and recorded in New York by the newly christened Mitch Ryder and the Detroit Wheels—Ryder might as well have been singing to a capacity crowd at Cobo Hall.

"You made me love you," he sang (not spoke). He strained, pushing for the notes and delivery that had made him famous. It was just a rehearsal, but Ryder seemed unable to stop himself from giving the vocal everything he had.

The band chimed in, bouncing background harmonies off basement walls. Ryder often said he does the same show for ten people that he does for ten thousand. That's an understatement. On a quiet summer night in suburban Detroit, Ryder took as much care and pride in his vocal performance as if Little Richard himself were in the otherwise empty basement.

The band worked with Ryder for three hours, a warm-up for the following night when he took the stage at a small-town movie theater, a benefit concert to restore a walking path in a senior-citizen community. Ryder performed for free, the band for the pleasure of playing with a Detroit music legend.

Included in the hundred or so shows Ryder performs each year are an impressive number of benefit concerts. In early 2005, the small town Ryder called home held a series of fund-raisers to help orphaned children in war-torn Sri Lanka whose fragile lives were further challenged by the December 26, 2004, Indian Ocean tsunami. He stepped up to the plate with a free performance and some autographed CDs to help raise funds.

When tickets for the show went on sale, Ryder was in the local newspaper office when the first of many fans came by to secure seats. "Hey, Mitch!" the surprised fan said. "How you doing?"

People were surprised to learn that Ryder was among their neighbors, living in one of the countless communities struggling to retain a rural identity on the fringes of a sprawling city. He's a part-time resident in many ways, dividing his time between Michigan and Germany, where he continued releasing CDs well into the twenty-first century, including the 2006 release *The Acquitted Idiot,* a multifaceted collection of songs hailed by musicians including Stewart Francke, who called it a "masterpiece."

With Robert Gillespie in Hamburg, Germany, January 2003. (Photo by Susan Scherer. Courtesy of Robert Gillespie.)

The songs are about redemption, about the human soul, about religion and trying to make peace with yourself. Not exactly the topics of a rock-and-roll record from 1966, but Ryder's life on the road taught lessons about far more than the allure of women wearing blue dresses.

Rather than slowing down after his sixtieth birthday had come and gone, Ryder seemed ready for a musical renaissance. While German audiences accepted the musical growth on the new CD, Ryder spent part of the summers of 2006 and 2007 as one of the headliners of "Hippiefest," a concert series with an eclectic lineup including Leslie West and Mountain, the Turtles, Felix Cavaliere (of the Young Rascals), the Zombies, Country Joe McDonald, and Melanie. These Sixties survivors were now playing before middle-aged audiences who sometimes brought grandchildren to their first-ever rock-and-roll show.

Whether playing a small-town theater or closing the Hippiefest show when it took the familiar stage of suburban Detroit's Pine Knob theater, Ryder is a familiar, welcome face to his fans. He sings the hits and enjoys

Gillespie jamming in Salzburg, Austria, January 2003. Off and on, Gillespie shared the stage more often with Ryder than any other musician, spanning from the early 1980s to the present. (Photo by Susan Scherer. Courtesy of Robert Gillespie.)

telling tales about the past. "Road stories," he calls them, some funny, others sad, always with a sense of perspective about fame in America. Ryder talked about a halftime appearance he made at a Detroit Pistons playoff game and seeing old friend and hometown hero Bob Seger seated just a few rows from the court. "Boy," he thought out loud, "I wish I could afford those seats."

The audience laughs, understands, and connects to the working-class sentiment that Ryder still embodies. Seger himself became a national star, and it's difficult to imagine Eminem, Kid Rock, or the White Stripes making claims of just being one of the crowd. Nobody would buy it, but Ryder is—and always has been—one of them.

In smaller venues, such as the local movie theater or at the annual Woodward Dream Cruise (a uniquely Detroit tradition of classic-car nostalgia and driving aimlessly up and down the iconic Avenue), Ryder spends time with fans, obliging autograph requests and posing for pictures next to people bearing an "I can't believe it" expression. Ryder gratefully listens to familiar stories.

"They tell me where they were the first time they heard a certain song, what they were doing," Ryder said. "Or they'll tell me about a specific concert they saw me at when that song was popular."

Four decades have gone by, entire lives played out with so much forgotten, but the fans know the chords, the lyrics, and the beat to "Jenny" and "Devil" as well as they know the year they graduated from high school. Maybe they're surprised that a three-minute rock-and-roll song holds more meaning for them than they might have thought. Inevitably the people get up and dance, and move, and celebrate something more than just a catchy tune. Ryder made it—survived the turbulent 1960s, the cynical 1970s, and the decades that followed—and so did the generation of Americans known as the baby boomers.

Ryder finished preparing the band for the benefit concert, giving it the same amount of attention paid to a crowded Pine Knob concert. The rehearsal in a suburban basement came to an end, and Ryder advised the musicians that any flaws in the performance should be overlooked.

"No matter what happens, just keep playing," Ryder said. "There will be some mistakes, but just keep playing."

He was referring to the concert, at which there were a few glitches, although nobody on the receiving end of the amplifiers noticed. The audience was too busy enjoying an intimate evening with a rock-and-roll star, the familiar voice heard forty years earlier on monophonic car speakers and transistor radios.

Singer-survivor: Ryder at work in 2007 during a concert to benefit a Sri Lankan orphanage. (Photo by Robert Alford.)

His advice was sound, though, and not just for musicians, wisdom learned the hard way over a nearly fifty-year career: set out to do something as well as possible, as good as you can make it. Try for perfection, if possible, but know that things don't always work out exactly as planned. When mistakes occur—and they will—work through them and try to do better next time.

"No matter what happens," Ryder said, "Just keep playing."

A MUSICAL
REVIEW

FEEDBACK

Other Voices

"I don't know what it is about Mitch Ryder," said Brian Wilson. "But he has one of the greatest voices in America." No small praise coming from the vocal mastermind of the Beach Boys, responsible for some of the most polished harmonies ever recorded.

The assessment of Mitch Ryder's voice and talent is a permanent impression, a legacy separate from sales figures (a measurement that often grants equal status to gimmicks, novelty acts, and one-hit wonders whose fame eclipsed their talent). Critics, fans, and other artists have long praised Ryder's basic abilities. Those same discussions inevitably include comment on a career that may have underachieved, given the talent and the voice being heard.

"At his peak, he was the white Wilson Pickett, one of the two or three greatest white soul singers ever to stalk the stage," said *Rolling Stone*'s Dave Marsh. "But Ryder is one of those rock-and-roll characters who got caught by fame in a transitional moment and never realized his due. If

["Devil" and "Jenny"] had been released a year sooner or five years later, Mitch Ryder might have become a superstar."

Ryder's is a familiar story of forever being linked to the sound that first brought fame. Bruce Conforth, original curator for the Rock and Roll Hall of Fame and Museum and professor of American culture at the University of Michigan, argued that producer Bob Crewe created a limited showcase for Ryder's abilities.

"I think Crewe more or less pigeonholed Mitch and didn't allow him to stretch the way he could have," said Conforth. "His talents are much broader. If people think of Mitch, they think of 'Devil with a Blue Dress On,' but Mitch is so much more than that, so much more complex."

Conforth said that "Devil" and the Wheels' primary hits were solid examples of classic rock and roll, but Ryder's voice should have been given greater respect. "Mitch was, as far as I'm concerned, the person who gave 'blue-eyed soul' its name," said Conforth. "If that term wasn't coined for him, it shouldn't have been coined for anyone."

The legacy of Mitch Ryder is arguably stronger in the home of the Detroit Wheels than it is nationwide, as was the amount of influence he provided not only fans but also future musicians. Detroit people are fiercely protective of their own.

"I was listening to the radio one night," said MC5 cofounder Wayne Kramer. "They said, 'There's a band from Detroit; you might have known them as Billy Lee and the Rivieras. They're now called Mitch Ryder and the Detroit Wheels.' They played 'Jenny Take a Ride.' It was so exciting to hear: that's my band; those are my guys! I discovered them! It seemed like everything blew up for them from there."

Kramer said the hits that followed "Jenny" provided certification that his favorite local stars were more than just regional idols to musically worship. "They were a great singles band," said Kramer, who by the time "Jenny" was a hit had formed his own group and felt hometown pride with a stronger motivation than most. "It absolutely confirmed for me that this was a realistic possibility. Maybe I could be a musician, have a cool band, and get my stuff on the radio one day."

Kramer knew that there was more to unlocking the vault of fame than just musical talent. Ryder was a showman who knew how to capture the audience's attention. Kramer's instinct told him that Ryder was behaving professionally in a business that only appeared to be casual and informal.

Promoter Russ Gibb agreed, recalling a musician who understood the work and protocol of a successful show. "The first time I heard Mitch Ryder, I didn't know who he was, but his voice . . . to this day . . . there's something about the roughness, a rough quality," Gibb said. "We were all from Detroit, called 'factory rats' when I was growing up. But his voice . . . 'Devil' still stands out, I still love it; it's a great tune. He had a great talent; he had . . . that voice."

Gibb joined others in questioning the career decisions that might have sounded good on paper. However, Bob Crewe's strategy to promote Ryder as a pop star in the Las Vegas tradition likely limited the singer's long-range career plans.

"He was influenced by the power in the record industry," Gibb said. "The big money was out in Las Vegas, and they were saying, 'Ahh, we got another one.' But his rhythm-and-blues roots were closer to what was going to happen than what he got involved in."

Gibb said Ryder was "a gentleman" in their dealings, ranging from Grande Ballroom gigs to the chaos of the Goose Lake Festival. Throughout the 1960s, Gibb watched pop singers become rock stars, complete with new attitudes that weren't always endearing.

"The rock thing was changing; they were becoming stars, becoming counterculture," Gibb said. "Mitch was a worker, don't kid yourself. Word passes around at the radio stations; we knew the guys who worked and the guys who lived off their reputations or were so doped up they didn't know what they were doing."

Gibb acknowledged that Ryder was no virgin when it came to the drug or alcohol abuse so common among the young and quickly famous. From an employer's standpoint, Gibb offered the most flattering complement any Detroit "factory rat" can hear: "He still gave a show. He was a professional."

Concert promoter and disc jockey Marilyn Bond agreed, both that Ryder could put on a show and that too much fame can threaten the ability to sustain the performance. "When you have fifteen-year-old kids in a candy store, what do they expect?" Bond said of the tempting offers put forth to young people, often from modest circumstances.

Of course, as Bond watched time and again, the free ride of fame is not always a long-term journey. "Then they snatch every single thing out from under them. What are they going to do? So many of them went into drugs and drinking and things like that at one time or another."

At the age of twenty, Ryder was thrust into the fickle lottery of American celebrity, uncertain of how he arrived at such a lofty place, less certain of how to keep his footing. Kramer, asked to wear a junior psychologist's hat, said that the rise to fame and arc of decline—sometimes self-generated—is a familiar story.

"There's a very common sequence of events for people who achieve a substantial amount of recognition at a very young age," Kramer said. "Being from the same kinds of neighborhoods [as Ryder], you have this sense that everything is going according to plan. Your band is successful and you're reaping all the rewards: You're getting all the sex you ever wanted; you're getting a nice car; you have some money to spend; and you're on television and on the radio. But it's a very precarious point at the top of a pyramid. It's hard to stay up there."

The inevitable fall from Grace, Kramer said, results from changing times, changing bands, and a public perpetually seeking newer faces and sounds. "The industry that gave you all those accolades moves on to someone else; they eat the young," Kramer said. "So now you're left trying to sustain a career, and you can't sustain it with the level of excitement and enthusiasm that you had before. A cynicism sets in; resentment starts to build. I'd say he fits that bill. I know I did, personally. I see a lot of me in him; we went through the same kinds of things."

The resentment and bitterness, Kramer said, is part—but hardly all—of the recipe that creates drug or alcohol problems.

"That's the point he might have been at, and I might have been entering, when we were trying to work together," Kramer said. "We both had this burden we were carrying around, and getting high was certainly a solution for it."

Wayne Gabriel shared Kramer's frustration of wondering if Ryder was underachieving in his career—twice. Gabriel was among the cast of Detroit that, regardless of lineup, seemed destined to remain a regional band; nearly a decade later, Gabriel was excited about the potential for a Ryder revival when he helped form the group that backed the singer in 1978. Gabriel, having spent part of the decade playing behind John Lennon and Bob Seger, thought the commercial potential existed for Ryder to make a run at the charts.

"I thought so much could happen with that band, but it just kept going nowhere," Gabriel said. "There were quite a few things that could have taken that band to the next level, but it never transpired." Gabriel was also enough of a veteran to know that talent is only one part in the formula for success and can be dominated by other factors such as management, decisions, and timing.

The willingness to seek fame is harder still to define and assess. "A lot of people with a lot of talent want the success," Gabriel said, "but they're also kind of scared of the success. A lot of that has to do with the innate destructiveness in a lot of artists. You keep going to see how far you can go, but you're also trying to keep yourself from having it."

The early comeback albums were not, Ryder insisted, an attempt at recapturing fame; instead, *How I Spent My Vacation* could be considered a declaration of artistic independence. Ryder knew the trappings of being a star and the uncertainty that came from flying solo, dating back to his handling by producer Bob Crewe.

"The most obvious thing I was aware of was that I was constantly being removed from the band," Ryder said of Crewe's focus on the lead singer. "But I didn't get an attitude about being a star. You know when I developed that attitude? When it was taken away from me. That's when I started saying, 'Hey, wait a minute. Don't you know who I was?'"

It would be one thing if Ryder—as many of the "here today, gone tomorrow" stars of the era—*had* ceased making records or performing new material in the years that followed his peak period of fame. By the time his comeback was complete and his career entered a third decade, Ryder was hardly relying on past glory while doing his job.

On the other hand, a pattern continued of opportunities that may have been better realized. When guitarist Robert Gillespie first joined Ryder in 1983, it appeared that the single "When You Were Mine" and *Never Kick a Sleeping Dog* album were opening the door for a career renaissance. "I thought it was happening," Gillespie said. "He could have made it big again."

Gillespie's is the most sustained perspective on Ryder's career, Wheels notwithstanding. Off and on, Gillespie spent nearly two decades sharing the stage with Ryder. "I've got eighteen years in," Gillespie noted, "Longer than anybody who hung out with him." The absence of a commercial follow-up to *Sleeping Dog,* Gillespie said, limited the impact it might have had in America, but Ryder's reputation overseas was not linked to either that album or the 1960s hits. German fans considered Ryder's Rockpalast music festival performance a classic, notable both for an inebriated noninterview before the show and the sensational performance that followed.

"He was just great, he was wonderful, and he was totally smashed," Gillespie said. "I've met so many kids—men, now—who never saw anybody that high on television before."

After more than a thousand performances together, Gillespie said he is still reminded on occasion of the power of Ryder's voice. "There have been times onstage when I've gotten chills," Gillespie said. "Those screams; it sounds like a vulture. I hear it on the monitors and just say, 'Wow, where did that come from.' I remember him doing 'Heart of Stone' at a European gig in 2002, and Mitch just knocked me out. I've heard him be absolutely breathtaking."

Harvey Ovshinsky, writer, filmmaker, and publisher in the Detroit area dating back to the late 1960s, said that Ryder's local hero status is not simply a matter of shared geographical roots. A true local hero remains loyal to those roots, Ovshinsky said, and Ryder embodied the blue-collar grit of the Motor City in a way that Motown's polished performers couldn't.

"Detroit has an amazing wealth of creative Karma," said Ovshinsky. "When we think of Mitch, there's a sense of pride and identity. We don't always thrive, don't always survive, but we're very good at what we do."

For Wayne Kramer, that quality born in the shadows of assembly lines comes with an ironic sense of stubborn individuality. "It was a matter of style as opposed to fashion," Kramer said of Ryder's musical legacy. "In his heart of hearts, he was a soul man. He was true to a style and aesthetic of music. Style is eternal; fashion is temporary. He wasn't trying to do whatever was the trend of the day; he was doing what he loved. He loved Little Richard, James Brown, and all that hard-edged rhythm-and-blues stuff, so he followed his interest and his heart, and it manifested itself in terms of style."

Fifty years after Mitch Ryder first gripped a microphone and sang to audiences, he reminds people in Detroit—and elsewhere—what the music was all about. Ryder concerts in twenty-first-century America often begin with his take on Lou Reed's "Rock and Roll." A raw electric guitar bounces out the opening notes; Ryder both sings and growls the lyric, infusing the words with meaning beyond the tribute to a musical genre he helped immortalize:

> *Then she turned on the Detroit station; couldn't believe she heard it at all;*
> *She started dancing to that fine, fine music;*
> *Her life was saved by rock and roll. . . .*

And it was all right.

ON THE RECORDS

An Oral Discography

Early in his career, Mitch Ryder learned through firsthand experience the value of titles and prestige in a culture perpetually in pursuit of self-admiration. On three occasions, Ryder and the Detroit Wheels were given the Grail-like gold record, the unconventional nature of which revealed the true nature of the business.

In most cases, the Recording Industry Association of America (RIAA) issued the ceremonial platter for records that produced one million dollars in sales. Producer Bob Crewe and his DynaVoice label, however, were not subscribing members of the organization; when sales dictated that some acknowledgment was due for the singles "Devil with a Blue Dress On," "Jenny Take a Ride," and "Sock It to Me—Baby," Crewe arranged for the band to receive an imitation of the prized RIAA disc.

"They had to give us a gold record," Ryder said. Specific reports of the total number of units sold were not available, but *Billboard* magazine's estimates certified that the records were at least comparable to those honored by the industry.

An unfortunate experiment of actually playing the souvenir determined two ironic results: "The needle peeled the gold paint off," Ryder said, the irony of an industry rife with masquerades not escaping him. Adding insult to injury, the recording itself was not the product of Mitch Ryder and the Detroit Wheels but was someone else's record with a Mitch Ryder label slapped on top.

It wasn't Ryder's first, and hardly his last, moment of lost musical innocence in a career spanning nearly half a century. William Levise Jr. began making records in 1962 with the single "Fool for You/That's the Way It's Going to Be." In 1964, Billy Lee and the Rivieras put their band's name on a pair of songs, "You Know" and "Won't You Dance with Me."

These were exciting times for the teenager who became Mitch Ryder; to have a 45-rpm recording of his own voice that could be played on the same turntable that brought the sounds of musical heroes into suburban bedrooms. An accomplishment, but with a short-lived sense of excitement given the lack of response or airplay. In 1965, under the name Mitch Ryder and the Detroit Wheels, fantasy became reality with the album *Take a Ride!*

"You hold it in your hands and can't deny the fact that you've made it," Ryder said. "You don't know how big it's going to get, but you know you accomplished something."

It was an achievement often repeated, some of which stood the test of time. (During a 2007 benefit concert, one fan came with a treasured copy of that very album to be autographed.) Some invite stronger memories than others, for both artist and audience.

In spite of a reputation built on a few songs, Ryder and his fans are equally surprised by the total number of recordings he made and impressed by the sustained dedication to a craft. There have been other recordings than those listed here: obscure compilations included a Canadian release, "Look Ma, No Wheels"; "Devil with the Blue Dress Off" was offered to Belgian audiences; and the satire "Good Golly, Ask Ollie" was issued in extended-single format. "Devil with a Blue Dress On" has appeared on countless soundtracks and compilations and remains Ryder's most often-played performance.

"After I'm gone, if somebody legitimately and honestly looks at my career, they'll see an artist who struggled to grow and achieve," Ryder said. "I've gotten fulfillment out of my music, and that's all you can really ask for."

TAKE A RIDE!   (1965, New Voice)
Mitch Ryder and the Detroit Wheels; produced by Bob Crewe

Shake a Tail Feather / Come See about Me / Let Your Love Light Shine / Just a Little Bit / I Hope / Jenny Take a Ride / Please, Please, Please / I'll Go Crazy / Got You (I Feel Good) / Sticks and Stones / Bring It On Home to Me / Baby Jane (*Mo-Mo Jane*) / I Don't Know

Sessions for the first LP by Mitch Ryder and the Detroit Wheels were sporadic, a precious hour or two squeezed in between shows and the obligations that come with trying to establish a rock-and-roll band. "Jenny Take a Ride" gave the group their first Top Ten hit and created the two-song format that became the band's signature. *Take a Ride!* included songs for which arrangements had been perfected onstage and also made room for tributes to musical influences, including "Shake a Tail Feather" and "Please, Please, Please," previously recorded by Ray Charles and James Brown.

"They were songs my heroes had created," Ryder said. "I wanted to be tested to see how I could perform against the originals."

In the case of "Jenny," the song became identified as much with Ryder as its originator, Little Richard. Rock writer Dave Marsh called the band's combination of "Jenny" with "C. C. Rider," an old blues tune by Chuck Willis, "maybe the most exciting white rock and roll anybody in America produced during the British Invasion."

BREAKOUT . . . !!!   (1966, New Voice)

Mitch Ryder and the Detroit Wheels; produced by Bob Crewe

Walking the Dog / I Had It Made / In the Midnight Hour / Ooh Poo Pah Doo / I Like It Like That / Little Latin Lupe Lu / Devil with a Blue Dress On/Good Golly, Miss Molly / Shakin' with Linda / Stubborn Kind of Fellow / You Get Your Kicks / I Need Help / Any Day Now / Breakout

The difference between the *Breakout . . . !!!* and *Take a Ride!* albums was more selection than progression. Ryder said the material came from recording sessions that put the band's stage repertoire on tape.

"These were things that didn't involve a lot of rehearsal time," Ryder said. Producer Bob Crewe saw little reason to tamper with the established sound, especially in the case of the two-song combination that had made "Jenny" a hit. For "Breakout," the mini-medley paired a Little Richard piece with a song written by Detroit soul singer Shorty Long, resulting in "Devil with a Blue Dress On/Good Golly, Miss Molly." Forget the "one-hit wonder" label; Ryder and the Wheels confirmed their position with their second Top Ten single.

"On the basis of this record," Marsh wrote in *Rolling Stone,* "the Detroit Wheels were one of the greatest rock bands ever."

Marsh acknowledged, however, "Much of the music wasn't made by the Wheels." Guest players on the album included Mike Bloomfield and future Electric Flag organist Barry Goldberg. The principal Wheels—drummer John Badanjek and guitarist Jimmy McCarty—were present and accounted for both on "Devil" and the album's first single, "Little Latin Lupe Lu," which Marsh placed at No. 450 in his collection of the top 1,001 singles in rock, a notch above the Righteous Brothers' recording from 1963.

"As for who did the greatest version," Marsh said, "You've gotta go with Mitch Ryder and the boys. It's one of those records you can never quite play loud enough."

Hints can be heard of producer Crewe separating the singer from the band, notably on "You Get Your Kicks" and the title song, "Breakout," which featured horns and a Big Band–type sound that tried to steer Ryder toward Crewe's beloved Las Vegas sound.

SOCK IT TO ME! (1967, New Voice)
Mitch Ryder and the Detroit Wheels; produced by Bob Crewe

Sock It to Me—Baby / I Can't Hide It / Takin' All I Can Get / Slow Fizz (instrumental) / Walk On By / I Never Had It Better / Shakedown / A Face in the Crowd / I'd Rather Go to Jail / Wild Child

For the third album, the backlog of songs from the band's stage arsenal was running dry, and producer Crewe scrambled for material.

"He was bringing in more original stuff and solo stuff," Ryder said. Of the ten songs, Crewe's name was credited as a songwriter on all but two, the Burt Bacharach–Hal David classic, "Walk On By," and "Shakedown," by Russell Brown and David Bloodworth.

By 1967, albums were no longer just a collection of smash hits or singles surrounded by "filler" songs chosen at random. Brian Wilson and the Beach Boys were putting the final touches on *Pet Sounds,* Bob Dylan's *Highway 61* had broken the length (and content) restrictions for "popular" songs, and the Beatles were warming up the orchestra for the release of *Sgt. Pepper's Lonely Hearts Club Band.*

Although not a concept album of lofty ambition, the recording sessions for *Sock It to Me!* were more intense than on the previous records. "It was very exciting, but it wasn't as easy as it had been prior to that," Ryder said. "It involved more homework on my part. We went from four to eight tracks, and some people were experimenting with stereo."

The result provided a milestone hit: "Sock It to Me—Baby" which continued the band's string of Top Forty pop records and topped the New York rhythm-and-blues sales charts, the first time for an all-white group. *Esquire* magazine's Robert Christgau discussed the album in an October

1967 review, "Secular Music—Soul Sounds," making the social-political argument that audiences remained somewhat segregated while artists tried to break the color barrier, not always with success.

"The old racism is still with us," said Christgau, but Ryder remained pure in his interpretations of black culture and music. "The popularity of singers like [Otis] Redding and [James] Brown has made possible a new kinds of sexual candor among white performers," Christgau continued. "Among these, I think Mitch Ryder is special. His stage presence is extraordinary."

Along with helping to bring the phrase "Sock it to me" to America, the album marked the last original recording credited to Mitch Ryder and the Detroit Wheels.

WHAT NOW MY LOVE   (1967, DynoVoice)
Mitch Ryder; produced by Bob Crewe

Let It Be Me / I Make a Fool of Myself / Born to Lose / If You Go Away / What Now My Love / Whole Lotta Shakin' / Sally Go 'Round the Roses / Brown Eyed Handsome Man / I Need Lovin' You / That's It, I Quit, I'm Movin' On

The album with the split personality: A polarized collection of songs providing a rock-and-roll showcase on one side and Crewe's more theatrical aspirations on the other.

"For me it was the challenge of singing whatever was tossed to me," Ryder said. "I wanted to be able to handle everything. It was a personal challenge."

Crewe assembled a talented cast of session players, including guitarist Bloomfield and drummer Freddy Purdy, and arguably put more effort into *What Now* than for what he considered pop records by the Wheels. "This was his defining moment," Ryder said of Crewe's ambitions. "He was going to make me a bona fide superstar or die trying."

Critics were at best confused and at times dismissive of the final product. The "A" side of lush arrangements, Rod McKuen poetry, and Vegas-lounge ballads contrasted with the straight-ahead rock, including a version of the Jerry Lee Lewis hit "Whole Lotta Shakin'.

The duality of the album signaled the end of Ryder's partnership with Crewe. Subsequent album releases were collections of two years' worth of studio sessions.

ALL MITCH RYDER HITS! (1967, New Voice) / **ALL THE HEAVY HITS** (1968, Crewe Records) / **MITCH RYDER SINGS THE HITS** (1968, New Voice)
Mitch Ryder; produced by Bob Crewe

Some call these compilation albums. The man whose name was on the cover had a different take on the products.

"Same shit in a different package," Ryder said. *All Mitch Ryder Hits!* and *All the Heavy Hits* (a limited release designed to highlight the single "I Never Had It Better") were pulled from the same well, being the three albums credited to Ryder and the Wheels. Both included the four principal hits: "Jenny Take a Ride," "Little Latin Lupe Lu," "Devil with a Blue Dress On," and "Sock It To Me—Baby." *Mitch Ryder Sings the Hits* featured the solo efforts of Ryder under Crewe's direction, released as singles or from the first side of *What Now My Love.*

THE DETROIT-MEMPHIS EXPERIMENT (1969, Dot Records, MCA, Repertoire Records)
Mitch Ryder; produced by Steve Cropper
Liberty / Eenie Meenie Minie Moe / Boredom / Push Aroun' / Sugar Bee / I Get Hot / I Believe / Direct Me / Long Long Time / Raise Your Hand / Wear and Tear on My Heart / Meat

Recorded at the famed Stax Records in Memphis, the *Experiment* featured the studio's longtime "house band," Booker T. and the MGs, under the direction of Steve Cropper, making his debut as a producer. With this *Experiment,* Ryder turned his back on the established hierarchy of the music business, both by rejecting the wave of psychedelic-inspired grooves and by featuring the extended-middle-finger liner notes that referred to his having been "raped" by the industry and declared Mitch Ryder "the sole creation of William Levise Jr."

"Liberty" may be the standout piece, a declaration of freedom by one of the first white artists to record at Stax. Although considered a "rush job" by Ryder, the album demonstrated more roots-oriented range than was allowed under Crewe's direction, from the gospel-influenced "I Believe" to the Wilson Pickett–worthy, "Push Aroun'."

DETROIT   (1971, Paramount)
Detroit . . . with Mitch Ryder; produced by Barry Kramer

Long Neck Goose / Is It You (Or Is It Me) / Box of Old Roses / It Ain't Easy / Rock and Roll / Let It Rock / Drink / Gimme Shelter / I Found a Love

A difficult record to record, with a somewhat unstable cast of characters, *Detroit* provided Ryder the opportunity to explore songwriting, with credits including "Is It You (Or Is It Me)" and "Drink." Ryder didn't ignore his rhythm-and-blues heritage and included a cover version of Wilson Pickett's "I Found a Love."

The band did not produce a chart-making single, although "Rock and Roll" was a regional FM favorite; the song remains a highlight of Ryder's stage show, as does the Rolling Stones anthem, "Gimme Shelter," which Ryder and his band expanded over the years to include an introductory medley of Stones songs.

The album ended the first phase of Ryder's career. A second Detroit LP never materialized, although Ryder continued to do shows until 1973, when the singer took a bow and headed west for a five-year absence from the spotlight.

GET OUT THE VOTE   (1997, Total Energy) *
Detroit . . . with Mitch Ryder; produced by John Sinclair

Little Bit of Love / Let It Rock / Can't Get Next to You; / Rock
and Roll / City Woman / C. C. Rider/Jenny Take a Ride / All in a
Dream / Rock and Roll Hootchie Koo / Gimme Shelter / Devil with a
Blue Dress On/Good Golly Miss Molly / Detroit Boogie
–* Recorded live in 1972–

An attempt to make a live concert recording and film by John Sinclair,
Get Out the Vote was an election-year project of high ambitions but a limited budget. "A cheap, one-microphone thing that John Sinclair created,"
Ryder said. "The liner notes were more about his political agenda, with
maybe two lines about the album."

Recorded during a political rally in Ann Arbor, Ryder delivered a
rough, energetic performance before leaving the stage. The classic Detroit
Wheels songs were included, along with material from the *Detroit* album
and cover versions including "Let It Rock," "Rock and Roll Hootchie Koo"
and the Motown hit "Can't Get Next to You."

HOW I SPENT MY VACATION   (1978, Seeds and Stems)
Mitch Ryder; produced by Tom Conner and Mitch Ryder

Tough Kid / Dance Ourselves to Death / Passions Wheel / Cherry
Poppin' / Freezin' in Hell / Nice 'n Easy / The Joy / Falling Forming / Poster

For the first time, Mitch Ryder put his art and soul into more than just the
vocals. Ryder crafted the album cover's painting and wrote the words and
music for a mini-biography of a "Tough Kid" (in the opening track) who
had been around the musical block.

"It was about trying to explain those years of exile," Ryder said. "People thought I'd dropped out of the business. I didn't have a choice. This
was a total, 100 percent effort to control every aspect of the music. Not so

much for ego, but for protection." Ryder formed the core of what would become his longest-running regular band, the Thrashing Brothers, including Wilson Owens, Wayne Gabriel, and Billy Csernits.

Sometimes misinterpreted, the autobiographical elements of *Vacation* were not intended for mass consumption. (A song inspired by John Sinclair, "The Joy" includes a *Little Red Book* reference for those who could connect the dots between the communist teachings of Chairman Mao Tse-Tung and the politically charged Sinclair.)

Vacation was the debut product of the Seeds and Stems record label formed by Ryder and Michigan producer Tom Conner. Independent deals were made for various regions of America, but the album was not picked up for mass-market distribution.

NAKED BUT NOT DEAD (1980, Seeds and Stems)
Mitch Ryder; produced by Tom Conner and Mitch Ryder

Ain't Nobody White / Corporate Song / War / The Future Looks Brite / I Got Mine / Spitting Lizard / True Love / I Don't Wanna to Hear It / Hometown

In many ways, *Naked But Not Dead* served as a sequel to *Vacation,* comprised in part from songs written in Colorado and continuing the relationship of Ryder and Conner as producers and business partners.

Ryder said the album featured less confessional songwriting than its predecessor, and portions of the album were intended to chase the "hook" of commercial success. On his own terms, Ryder was not opposed to exploring musical venues other than rhythm and blues or rock and roll.

"Having my own label was an opportunity to find out what I could do musically," Ryder said. "The Future Looks Bright" was written in the tradition of Broadway show tunes; "True Love" served up a reggae-flavored beat and cadence. Lyrically, Ryder recounted the story of a quote attributed to Ray Charles, "Ain't nobody white can sing the blues, except the Jews." Singer Elvis Costello criticized the comment, which earned him the wrath of Bonnie Delaney and a lyric from Ryder.

"It was still an American album," Ryder said. "I was trying to experiment with different forms. If I'd felt like doing an operetta, I would have."

Naked But Not Dead did not feature any soprano arias, but Ryder caught the ear of German producer and arranger Uwe Tessnow, head of Line Records. A distribution package deal was made for both *Vacation* and *Naked* for European release.

GOT CHANGE FOR A MILLION?   (1981, Line Records)
Mitch Ryder; produced by Tom Conner and Mitch Ryder

My Heart Belongs to Me / Back at Work / That's Charm / Red Scar Eyes / Bang Bang / Betty's Too Tight / Ich Bin Aus Amerika / Bare Your Soul / We're Gonna Win

In 1982, Ryder was nominated as Best New Artist by a German music association for *Got Change for a Million?* recorded in Hamburg. Two cuts, however, were recorded in the United States with emerging producer Don Was: "Bare Your Soul" and "We're Gonna Win." Continued experimentation was heard on some songs, but "Betty's Too Tight" was classic rock and roll, and "My Heart Belongs to Me" was pure rhythm and blues.

Recording sessions of the 1980s were far more complicated than the hurry-up-and-tape-it style of the 1960s, and Ryder balanced recording time with a full itinerary of concert performances. Studio time for the album came on the heels of a lengthy tour of Europe, and Ryder felt the weight of wearing so many hats.

"I was realizing my dream of a kid in the candy shop," Ryder said. "But we had just done a friggin' seven-week tour, and we only had ten days to record." Ryder said he took the role of producer, arranger, and writer, along with other, unofficial duties: "I had to be the cheerleader, morale keeper, coach, and referee. It was a good lesson for me down the road: I learned how to be prepared, to minimize my mistakes."

LIVE TALKIES (1981, Line Records, J-Bird)

Mitch Ryder; produced by Tom Conner and Mitch Ryder

It's All Over Now / Corporate Song / Bang Bang / Subterranean Homesick Blues / Wicked Messenger / Er Ist Nicht Mein President / Take Me to the River / Tough Kid / Red Scar Eyes; / Long Tall Sally/I'm Gonna Be a Wheel Someday / Liberty / Ain't Nobody White / Nice 'n Easy / True Love

Ryder called *Live Talkies* a combination of the concert recording and studio work, a frenzied, don't-stop performance of a band wired in more ways than one. The performance was memorable as much for what wasn't on tape as the final product.

"Everybody was amazingly high," Ryder said. "There were two fights in the studio. The keyboard player had a cast on his leg; he fell down in Paris from a heroin-induced coma and broke his leg. He was treating the pain with heroin, and the drummer got into a fight with him, attacking this poor guy who's got a cast on his leg."

Everybody jumped into the free-for-all, which lasted about fifteen minutes, Ryder said, before musicians retreated to their respective corners of the studio. Within a few minutes, they were recording again, songs ranging from throughout Ryder's career. (The absence of Detroit Wheels hits is made up for with the classic rocker "Long Tall Sally.") An inspired instrumental backing made for an interesting translation of Bob Dylan's "Subterranean Homesick Blues," and the two-disc release included "Liberty" from the Detroit-Memphis album. Ryder's growing comfort with the German language included "Er Ist Nicht Mein President" (He is not my President), which Ryder said was both a critique of Ronald Reagan and fearful speculation of a possible George H. W. Bush presidency.

SMART ASS (1982, Line Records)

Mitch Ryder; produced by Mitch Ryder

Hot House / You Better Stop It / Try and Must / Code Dancing / Tape's Rolling / One Room World / Hands High / It Keeps You Alive / Berlin

From a business standpoint, *Smart Ass* was Mitch Ryder's first true solo flight, because he was now serving as the lone producer and writing or cowriting each of the songs. Thrashing Brothers Billy Csernits and Mark Gougeon retained their roles in the band, now joined by guitarists Joe Gutc and Rick Schein and drummer Al Wotton. The album's engineer, Rick Kerr, was also a drummer. Curiously, Ryder said, "What you hear most is the drums."

Detroit-area fans who carefully read the credits recognized one of the songwriters for "One Room World," Ernie Harwell, the longtime Detroit Tigers announcer. Harwell and Ryder wrote the lyrics for a sad tale of an elderly lady resigned to live out her life in the title confines. (Harwell self-mockingly called it "the biggest no-hitter" he'd ever seen.)

NEVER KICK A SLEEPING DOG (1983, Polygram)

Mitch Ryder; produced by John Mellencamp (credited as "Little Bastard")

B.I.G. T.I.M.E. / When You Were Mine / A Thrill's a Thrill / Come Again / Cry to Me / The Thrill of It All / Stand / Rue de Tra-hir / Code Dancing

Mellencamp was part of a back-to-basics, "American sound" style. Add to that mix the songwriting of Prince, the veteran voice of Sixties survi-vor Marianne Faithful, and the backbeat of Eighties girl-group drummer Gina Shock—and the result is a sometimes polished, often raw workshop of American rock and roll.

"This is what John [Mellencamp] viewed as commercial," Ryder said. Mellencamp wasn't alone. Polygram Records provided what Ryder hadn't had since the Detroit Wheels albums—a legitimate promotion and marketing effort by an American label. The single "When You Were Mine" brought Ryder back to the contemporary market, including a video produced for MTV. Ryder and Mellencamp performed a duet of the rocker, "B.I.G. T.I.ME.," at the American Music Awards. Ryder continued his songwriting on the album, including "Come Again," a joint venture with Mellencamp, along with "The Thrill of It All" and "Stand."

Released on June 17, 1983, *Never Kick a Sleeping Dog* cracked the *Billboard* magazine Top 200 for album sales (peaking at No. 121), and the single "When You Were Mine" reached No. 85 on the singles chart. In spite of respectable sales, Polygram declined to exercise its option for a second album.

IN THE CHINA SHOP   (1986, Line Records)
Mitch Ryder; produced by Mitch Ryder

Where Is the Next One Comin' From? / Like a Worm / Rock-n-Roll Skin / All the Way / Looks Are Deceiving / I'm Not Sad Tonite / End of the Line / Uncle Sam and the Russian Bear / Youngblood / Everybody Loses

Ryder didn't spend too much time chasing the American market hinted at with *Sleeping Dog,* and continued building a studio-and-performing career in Germany. Recording sessions were balanced against a steady European concert schedule. Ryder refocused his songwriting efforts for *In the China Shop,* which also included a piece by veteran blues man John Hiatt, "Where Is the Next One Comin' From?" Most of the album's pieces were original compositions, though.

"The rest told personal stories," Ryder said. "There was an attempt to clean things up to get a better sound and become more competitive."

LEGENDARY FULL MOON CONCERT (1985, Line Records) / **RED BLOOD, WHITE MINK** (1988, Line Records) / **THE BEAUTIFUL TOULANG SUNSET** (1990, Line Records)

Mitch Ryder; produced by Mitch Ryder

"Live" and compilation records were periodically released, usually avoiding the 1960s hits in favor of the songs European audiences identified with Ryder, including "Ain't Nobody White," "Freezin' in Hell" and a cover of a Doors song, "Soul Kitchen." *Toulang Sunset* included one original song, "Junkie Love." Only the live album, *Red Blood, White Mink* (filmed for broadcast in Eastern bloc countries), expanded the repertoire back far enough to include "Little Latin Lupe Lu" and "Rock and Roll."

Ryder said the prevailing attitude for the ambitious East Germany concert was, "We can do rock and roll as good as the West," and they were supportive of the respected talent. It was an ambitious show, with huge screens, the best technicians, and professional staff, but there was one problem.

"What they didn't have was a sober artist," Ryder said of his vodka days. The recorded performance was never aired in the West, although the album captured the energetic show that earned respectable reviews in Germany.

LA GASH (1992, Line Records)

Mitch Ryder; produced by Mitch Ryder

It Must Be in Her Genes / Argyle / Do You Feel Alright / Child of Rage / Bye Bye Love / Dr. Margaret Smith / It's Your Birthday / Arms Without Love / Correct Me If I'm Wrong / One Thing / Almost Bigamy / Terrorist

Ryder called *La Gash* an album about his personal love life, with songs either about or cowritten with his wife. It wasn't the only topic, however: "Correct Me If I'm Wrong" offered a statement about abortion, and politics were at the forefront of "Terrorist." Ryder's wife cowrote "Dr. Margaret Smith," the story of the radio psychologist she portrayed on *Mitch Ryder's Radio Playhouse.*

Although writing more, Ryder surrendered his publishing rights to the songs on *La Gash* in exchange for a more sizeable budget for the studio production. "In order to record in a good studio, with a good budget, they demanded I give up my publishing," Ryder said. "It was a trade-off; I wanted to make a good record."

RITE OF PASSAGE   (1994, Line Records)
Mitch Ryder; produced by Mitch Ryder and Matthia Haertl.

See Her Again / Sex You Up / Actually 101 / It Wasn't Me / We Are Helpless / Into the Blue / Mercy / Too Sentimental / Let It Shine / Herman's Garden / I'm Startin' All Over Again / By the Feel

In Ryder's self-assessment, his musical mission began achieving its goals with the album *Rite of Passage.*

"This brought me to a place equal to *How I Spent my Vacation.* There was a lot of thought to it," Ryder said. "I was getting closer than ever to becoming really good at writing and production . . . but still falling short of the mark."

Ryder called the album experimental, with a jazz song, some blues tunes, and the pop-oriented "See Her Again" which he sent to doo-wop rocker Huey Lewis for possible consideration as a Huey Lewis and the News recording. Lewis declined to record the song but called Ryder to praise the work. "He told me he understood why I thought it might be a Huey Lewis song," Ryder said. "It couldn't have been more pop-ish."

The song "Mercy" and its connection to assisted-suicide advocate Dr. Jack Kevorkian briefly returned Ryder to the American public's attention. Rather than inspire debate, the controversy surrounding the song limited its commercial potential, but Ryder considered the work an accomplishment.

"It was an important album," Ryder said of *Rite of Passage*, but not the one to complete the marriage of artistic freedom and commercial exposure.

MONKEY ISLAND   (1999, Line Records)
Mitch Ryder; produced by Mitch Ryder

Monkey Island / Learning Cha Cha / Jackpot / Don't Go Back / Hello Willie / Market / Who Are You? / Remember / I'm in Denial / Roman Holiday / Thirteen Islands of Monkey Island

Ryder worked on *Monkey Island* with lyrics and melodies to accompany some experimental recordings that he called "industrial music." The album may not have been his best work, Ryder said, but it was among the hardest to produce.

"The level of creativity that was required was the highest that's ever been demanded of me," Ryder said. Admittedly "a difficult album to embrace," there were memorable moments. "Market" remains in his stage act today, and as a writer Ryder addressed racism in "Hello Willie," and pondered the attempt by some blacks to surrender their cultural heritage to suburban America in "Don't Go Back."

THE OLD MAN SPRINGS A BONER (2003, Line Records)
Mitch Ryder; produced by Mitch Ryder

War / Freezin' in Hell / Ain't Nobody White / Heart of Stone / Wicked Messenger / Red Scar Eyes / True Love / Gimme Shelter / Soul Kitchen

A live concert album as notable for the stage energy it captured of a singer approaching his sixthieth birthday as for the blunt title. "We did some live takes on songs that were particularly inspiring," Ryder said. "For a gentleman of my chronological age, I thought it was an appropriate title."

The Old Man included recordings from five shows in Germany, con-

tinuing a European preference for more contemporary songs over Detroit
Wheels hits.

A DARK CAUCASIAN BLUE   (2004, BuschFunk)
Mitch Ryder; produced by Mitch Ryder

Yeah You Right / From a Buick 6 / I Guess I'm Feeling Blue / Detroit
(By the River) / The Porch / Maikaefer Fliege / The New Mother /
Just One More Beautiful Day / Dear Lord Won't You Help This
Child / Another Bout with Justice / Decidedly British Blues / How
How How How (The Spider Gets Hungry)

In the first album produced for BuschFunk—a German record label that
not only allowed but also encouraged Ryder's musical explorations—Ryder produced a concept album of sorts, on a subject he now qualified as
an authority. "It primarily deals with the blues, in one form or another,
rhythm and blues," Ryder said. "I go back to my roots with this album."

Arguably, "Decidedly British Blues" was Ryder's most ambitious attempt yet, putting words to a melody by Ludwig van Beethoven. "I was
of the mind that, if the blues had existed, he would have called it a blues
song," Ryder said of the melody.

THE ACQUITTED IDIOT   (2006, Buschfunk)
Mitch Ryder; produced by Mitch Ryder

If You Need the Pain / Last Night / The Testament / Don't U Lie /
It's Broken / Star Nomore / Nobody Hates You / What We Believe /
You Taught Me How to Cry / Say Goodbye / The Wishlist / Hit 'n Run
Lover

Ryder called *The Acquitted Idiot* his masterpiece, where his talents came
together in a unified, sustained performance. That opinion was not restricted to the vanity of the artist.

"He's among the three best singers I've ever heard in my life," wrote Stewart Francke on his September 2006 web log. "Not only have his chops remained; he now has a bittersweet falsetto and a low end that can finish a phrase with stunning emotion."

Francke called the album Ryder's return to a, "spiritual and musical home" that combines the best elements of blues, rhythm and blues, and gospel. Francke compared the album's scope to the 2006 Bob Dylan release *Modern Times*" and said Ryder was long overdue for a career-spanning sense of respect.

"That's where I put Mitch—up with his peers, writing and singing and making records on par with Dylan, Bruce, Seger, or even Sam Moore and Jerry Lee Lewis," Francke wrote. "He's not resting; he's relevant, continually making new work, reinventing his own reinventions."

The album included a range of expressions, from the old-school rhythm and blues on "Last Night" to the mariachi-flavored prayer, "What We Believe." "The Testament" pays tribute to one-time duet partner Otis Redding, and Ryder's new vocal is heard over tapes recorded in the late 1960s by the Funk Brothers, the principal group of players for Motown (a band given their due in the documentary *Standing in the Shadows of Motown*).

Getting the right elements together at the right time was as much a personal triumph for Ryder as an artistic statement. "Nobody can tell me anymore that I was a manufactured star from Bob Crewe," Ryder said, an image that haunted him for four decades. "That was my goal, and I did it."

That didn't mean the artist was prepared to retire.

"Now, if I'm allowed to," Ryder said, "I'll try to make something equal to it or better. That's a hell of a challenge."

SELECTED BIBLIOGRAPHY

This bibliography is not a complete record of all the sources consulted.
I list here only the most important materials relevant to this book.

NEWSPAPERS, MAGAZINE ARTICLES, WEBSITES, MEDIA

Badalament, Steve. Interview with Johnny Badanjek. *Classic Drummer*, October 2005.

Burnstein, Jay. World Trade Center interview. Official Mitch Ryder Website, August 28, 2001, http://www.mitchryder.de.

Blue, Buddy. "Chrissie Hynde: She's No Pretender." *San Diego Union-Tribune*, March 23, 2006.

Christgau, Robert. "Secular Music" (review of *Sock It to Me!*). *Esquire*, October 1967.

Cioe, Crispin McCormick. "Mitch Ryder: Return with us to the days when rock reigned, and get ready—he's gonna bring it all back." *Detroit Magazine (Free Press)*, March 4, 1979.

"Court Ruling Keeps Death Penalty Ban." *Detroit News*, July 24, 1982.

"Death Penalty Lawsuit to Be Heard . . ." *Detroit Free Press*, July 15, 1982.

Detroit Free Press. Goose Lake festival: articles week of August 7–9, 1970.

Dominic, Serene. "The Ryder Stipulates." *Metro Times,* September 15, 2004.

"For the Record." WDIV-TV special, 1983, produced/hosted by Tim Coleman.

Francke, Stewart. Review of *The Acquitted Idiot.* Stewart Francke.com (blog), September 2006, http://www.stewartfrancke.com.

"Hot 100 Stars: Biography on Release of "Devil." *Billboard,* October 15, 1966.

Interview with Mitch Ryder. Blasting-Zone.com, July 2003, http://www.blasting-zone.com.

Loder, Kurt. "Mitch Ryder's Final Fling." *Rolling Stone,* September 1, 1983.

Marsh, Dave. Review of *Naked But Not Dead. Rolling Sto*ne, August 7, 1980.

"Matt Beer's Sunday Brunch." *Detroit Free Press/News,* April 8, 1984.

McFarlin, Jim. "Ryder Rides Again." *Detroit News,* July 15, 1983.

McGrath, Rick. "Rock 'n' Roll: The Mitch Ryder Interview." *Georgia Straight,* July 1970

"Mitch Ryder, at Palace Theater in Canton, Ohio." Lairdslair.com, November 21, 1998.

"Mitch Ryder, Naked But Not Dead." *Cucamonga* (Belgian television and radio website), 2003 interviews, http://www.cucamonga.be.

"Musicians Recall First Heard Music." *Detroit News (*reprint from *Hartford [Conn.] Courant),* December 21, 1984.

Palmer, Robert. "From Detroit to Fame." The Pop Life, *New York Times,* June 29, 1983.

Review of reunion concert at Pine Knob. *Detroit News,* July 23, 1984.

Rockpalast archives concert review, Alan Bangs interview, discography. June 1979.

"Ryder Cancels Show after State Fair Bans Song." *Detroit News,* August 17, 1994.

"Ryder 1st on Walk of Fame." *Detroit News,* March 2, 1989.

"Ryder's New Wheels." *Detroit News,* July 20, 1984.

Shimamato, Ken. Interview with Ron Cooke (bassist for Detroit). I-94 Bar (Australian e-zine), October 2000, http://www.i94bar.com.

"Suicide Crusade Proceeds from 'Mercy' to Kevorkian." *Detroit News,* March 22, 1994.

Trowbridge, Chris. "Mitch Ryder: Doctor Detroit." *Eye Weekly,* November 28, 2002.

Ward, Ed. "In Detroit: Mitch Ryder, No Wheels" *Rolling Stone,* March 2, 1972.

Werbe, Peter. Interview with Jim McCarty. *Vintage Guitar,* May 1999.

BOOKS

Carson, David A. *Grit, Noise, and Revolution: The Birth of Detroit Rock n Roll.* Ann Arbor: University of Michigan Press, 2005.

Lewisohn, Mark. *The Beatles: 25 Years in the Life*. London: Sedgwick and Jackson, 1987.

Marsh, Dave. *The Heart of Rock & Soul: The 1001 Greatest Singles Ever Made*. New York: New American Library, 1989.

Posner, Gerald L. *Motown: Music, Money, Sex, and Power*. New York: Random House, 2002.

Torgoff, Martin. *American Fool: The Roots and Improbable Rise of John Cougar Mellencamp*. New York: St. Martin's, 1986.

Whitburn, Joel. *The Billboard Book of Top 40 Hits*. North Hollywood, Calif.: Billboard Directories, 1996.

RELATED INFORMATION

National Institute on Media and the Family (statistics of television ownership), http://www.mediafamily.org.

Official Mitch Ryder Website bio, http://www.mitchryder.de.

Rock and Roll Hall of Fame Museum inductee biographies, Elvis Presley, Little Richard, James Brown, Jimi Hendrix, http://www.rockhall.com.

Songwriters Hall of Fame Bio on Bob Crewe, http://www.songwritershalloffame.org.

INDEX